The Faerie Queene by Edmund Spenser

Book IV. The Legend of Cambel and Triamond

THE SECOND PART OF THE FAERIE QUEENE CONTAINING THE FOURTH, FIFTH, AND SIXTH BOOKES

THE FOURTH BOOKE OF THE FAERIE QUEENE CONTAINING THE LEGEND OF CAMBEL AND TRIAMOND OR OF FRIENDSHIP

One of the greatest of English poets, Edmund Spenser was born in East Smithfield, London, in 1552. He was educated in London at the Merchant Taylors' School and later at Pembroke College, Cambridge. In 1579, he published The Shepheardes Calender, his first major work.

Edmund journeyed to Ireland in July 1580, in the service of the newly appointed Lord Deputy, Arthur Grey, 14th Baron Grey de Wilton. His time included the terrible massacre at the Siege of Smerwick.

The epic poem, The Faerie Queene, is acknowledged as Edmund's masterpiece. The first three books were published in 1590, and a second set of three books were published in 1596.

Indeed the reality is that Spenser, through his great talents, was able to move Poetry in a different direction. It led to him being called a Poet's Poet and brought rich admiration from Milton, Raleigh, Blake, Wordsworth, Keats, Byron, and Lord Tennyson, among others.

Spenser returned to Ireland and in 1591, Complaints, a collection of poems that voices complaints in mournful or mocking tones was published.

In 1595, Spenser published Amoretti and Epithalamion. The volume contains eighty-nine sonnets.

In the following year Spenser wrote a prose pamphlet titled A View of the Present State of Ireland, a highly inflammatory argument for the pacification and destruction of Irish culture.

On January 13th 1599 Edmund Spenser died at the age of forty-six. His coffin was carried to his grave in Westminster Abbey by other poets, who threw many pens and pieces of poetry into his grave followed with many tears.

Index of Contents
Book IV. The Legend of Cambel and Triamond
Introductory verses
Canto I
Canto II
Canto III
Canto IV
Canto V
Canto VI
Canto VII
Canto VIII
Canto IX
Canto X
Canto XI

Canto XII
Edmund Spenser – A Short Biography
Edmund Spenser – A Concise Bibliography

INTRODUCTORY VERSES

I
The rugged forhead that with grave foresight
Welds kingdomes causes and affaires of state,
My looser rimes (I wote) doth sharply wite,
For praising love, as I have done of late,
And magnifying lovers deare debate;
By which fraile youth is oft to follie led,
Through false allurement of that pleasing baite,
That better were in vertues discipled,
Then with vaine poemes weeds to have their fancies fed.

II
Such ones ill judge of love, that cannot love,
Ne in their frosen hearts feele kindly flame:
Forthy they ought not thing unknowne reprove,
Ne naturall affection faultless blame,
For fault of few that have abusd the same.
For it of honor and all vertue is
The roote, and brings forth glorious flowres of fame,
That crowne true lovers with immortall blis,
The meed of them that love, and do not live amisse.

III
Which who so list looke backe to former ages,
And call to count the things that then were donne,
Shall find, that all the workes of those wise sages,
And brave exploits which great heroes wonne,
In love were either ended or begunne:
Witnesse the father of philosophie,
Which to his Critias, shaded oft from sunne,
Of love full manie lessons did apply,
The which these Stoicke censours cannot well deny.

IV
To such therefore I do not sing at all,
But to that sacred saint my soveraigne Queene,
In whose chast breast all bountie naturall
And treasures of true love enlocked beene,
Bove all her sexe that ever yet was seene:
To her I sing of love, that loveth best
And best is lov'd of all alive, I weene;
To her this song most fitly is addrest,
The queene of love, and prince of peace from heaven blest.

V
Which that she may the better deigne to heare,
Do thou, dred infant, Venus dearling dove,
From her high spirit chase imperious feare,
And use of awfull majestie remove:
In sted thereof with drops of melting love,
Deawd with ambrosiall kisses, by thee gotten
From thy sweete smyling mother from above,
Sprinckle her heart, and haughtie courage soften,
That she may hearke to love, and reade this lesson often.

CANTO I

Fayre Britomart saves Amoret:
Duessa discord breedes
Twixt Scudamour and Blandamour:
Their fight and warlike deedes.

I
Of lovers sad calamities of old
Full many piteous stories doe remaine,
But none more piteous ever was ytold,
Then that of Amorets hart-binding chaine,
And this of Florimels unworthie paine:
The deare compassion of whose bitter fit
My softened heart so sorely doth constraine,
That I with teares full oft doe pittie it,
And oftentimes doe wish it never had bene writ.

II
For from the time that Scudamour her bought
In perilous fight, she never joyed day;
A perilous fight when he with force her brought
From twentie knights, that did him all assay:
Yet fairely well he did them all dismay,
And with great glorie both the Shield of Love
And eke the ladie selfe he brought away;
Whom having wedded, as did him behove,
A new unknowen mischiefe did from him remove.

III
For that same vile enchantour Busyran,
The very selfe same day that she was wedded,
Amidst the bridale feast, whilest every man,
Surcharg'd with wine, were heedlesse and ill hedded,
All bent to mirth before the bride was bedded,

Brought in that Mask of Love which late was showen:
And there the ladie ill of friends bestedded,
By way of sport, as oft in maskes is knowen,
Conveyed quite away to living wight unknowen.

IV
Seven moneths he so her kept in bitter smart,
Because his sinfull lust she would not serve,
Untill such time as noble Britomart
Released her, that else was like to sterve,
Through cruell knife that her deare heart did kerve.
And now she is with her upon the way,
Marching in lovely wise, that could deserve
No spot of blame, though spite did oft assay
To blot her with dishonor of so faire a pray.

V
Yet should it be a pleasant tale, to tell
The diverse usage, and demeanure daint,
That each to other made, as oft befell.
For Amoret right fearefull was and faint,
Lest she with blame her honor should attaint,
That everie word did tremble as she spake,
And everie looke was coy and wondrous quaint,
And everie limbe that touched her did quake:
Yet could she not but curteous countenance to her make.

VI
For well she wist, as true it was indeed,
That her lives lord and patrone of her health
Right well deserved, as his duefull meed,
Her love, her service, and her utmost wealth:
All is his justly, that all freely dealth.
Nathlesse her honor, dearer then her life,
She sought to save, as thing reserv'd from stealth;
Die had she lever with enchanters knife,
Then to be false in love, profest a virgine wife.

VII
Thereto her feare was made so much the greater
Through fine abusion of that Briton mayd:
Who, for to hide her fained sex the better
And maske her wounded mind, both did and sayd
Full many things so doubtfull to be wayd,
That well she wist not what by them to gesse;
For other whiles to her she purpos made
Of love, and otherwhiles of lustfulnesse,
That much she feard his mind would grow to some excesse.

VIII
His will she feard; for him she surely thought

To be a man, such as indeed he seemed,
And much the more, by that he lately wrought,
When her from deadly thraldome he redeemed,
For which no service she too much esteemed:
Yet dread of shame and doubt of fowle dishonor
Made her not yeeld so much as due she deemed.
Yet Britomart attended duly on her,
As well became a knight, and did to her all honor.

IX
It so befell one evening, that they came
Unto a castell, lodged there to bee,
Where many a knight, and many a lovely dame,
Was then assembled, deeds of armes to see:
Amongst all which was none more faire then shee,
That many of them mov'd to eye her sore.
The custome of that place was such, that hee
Which had no love nor lemman there in store
Should either winne him one, or lye without the dore.

X
Amongst the rest there was a jolly knight,
Who, being asked for his love, avow'd
That fairest Amoret was his by right,
And offred that to justifie alowd.
The warlike virgine, seeing his so prowd
And boastfull chalenge, wexed inlie wroth,
But for the present did her anger shrowd;
And sayd, her love to lose she was full loth,
But either he should neither of them have, or both.

XI
So foorth they went, and both together giusted;
But that same younker soone was over throwne,
And made repent that he had rashly lusted
For thing unlawfull, that was not his owne:
Yet since he seemed valiant, though unknowne,
She, that no lesse was courteous then stout,
Cast how to salve, that both the custome showne
Were kept, and yet that knight not locked out;
That seem'd full hard t' accord two things so far in dout.

XII
The seneschall was cal'd to deeme the right:
Whom she requir'd, that first fayre Amoret
Might be to her allow'd, as to a knight
That did her win and free from chalenge set:
Which straight to her was yeelded without let.
Then, since that strange knights love from him was quitted,
She claim'd that to her selfe, as ladies det,
He as a knight might justly be admitted;

So none should be out shut, sith all of loves were fitted.

XIII
With that, her glistring helmet she unlaced;
Which doft, her golden lockes, that were up bound
Still in a knot, unto her heeles downe traced,
And like a silken veile in compasse round
About her backe and all her bodie wound:
Like as the shining skie in summers night,
What time the dayes with scorching heat abound,
Is creasted all with lines of firie light,
That it prodigious seemes in common peoples sight.

XIV
Such when those knights and ladies all about
Beheld her, all were with amazement smit,
And every one gan grow in secret dout
Of this and that, according to each wit:
Some thought that some enchantment faygned it;
Some, that Bellona in that warlike wise
To them appear'd, with shield and armour fit;
Some, that it was a maske of strange disguise:
So diversely each one did sundrie doubts devise.

XV
But that young knight, which through her gentle deed
Was to that goodly fellowship restor'd,
Ten thousand thankes did yeeld her for her meed,
And, doubly overcommen, her ador'd:
So did they all their former strife accord;
And eke fayre Amoret, now freed from feare,
More franke affection did to her afford,
And to her bed, which she was wont forbeare,
Now freely drew, and found right safe assurance theare.

XVI
Where all that night they of their loves did treat,
And hard adventures, twixt themselves alone,
That each the other gan with passion great
And griefull pittie privately bemone.
The morow next, so soone as Titan shone,
They both uprose, and to their waies them dight:
Long wandred they, yet never met with none
That to their willes could them direct aright,
Or to them tydings tell that mote their harts delight.

XVII
Lo! thus they rode, till at the last they spide
Two armed knights, that toward them did pace,
And each of them had ryding by his side
A ladie, seeming in so farre a space;

But ladies none they were, albee in face
And outward shew faire semblance they did beare;
For under maske of beautie and good grace
Vile treason and fowle falshood hidden were,
That mote to none but to the warie wise appeare.

XVIII
The one of them the false Duessa hight,
That now had chang'd her former wonted hew:
For she could d'on so manie shapes in sight,
As ever could cameleon colours new;
So could she forge all colours, save the trew.
The other no whit better was then shee,
But that, such as she was, she plaine did shew;
Yet otherwise much worse, if worse might bee,
And dayly more offensive unto each degree.

XIX
Her name was Ate, mother of debate
And all dissention, which doth dayly grow
Amongst fraile men, that many a publike state
And many a private oft doth overthrow.
Her false Duessa, who full well did know
To be most fit to trouble noble knights,
Which hunt for honor, raised from below
Out of the dwellings of the damned sprights,
Where she in darkness wastes her cursed daies and nights.

XX
Hard by the gates of hell her dwelling is,
There whereas all the plagues and harmes abound,
Which punish wicked men, that walke amisse.
It is a darksome delve farre under ground,
With thornes and barren brakes environd round,
That none the same may easily out win;
Yet many waies to enter may be found,
But more to issue forth when one is in:
For discord harder is to end then to begin.

XXI
And all within, the riven walls were hung
With ragged monuments of times forepast,
All which the sad effects of discord sung:
There were rent robes and broken scepters plast,
Altars defyl'd, and holy things defast,
Disshivered speares, and shields ytorne in twaine,
Great cities ransackt, and strong castles rast,
Nations captived, and huge armies slaine:
Of all which ruines there some relicks did remaine.

XXII

There was the signe of antique Babylon,
Of fatall Thebes, of Rome that raigned long,
Of sacred Salem, and sad Ilion,
For memorie of which on high there hong
The golden apple, cause of all their wrong,
For which the three faire goddesses did strive:
There also was the name of Nimrod strong,
Of Alexander, and his princes five,
Which shar'd to them the spoiles that he had got alive:

XXIII

And there the relicks of the drunken fray,
The which amongst the Lapithees befell:
And of the bloodie feast, which sent away
So many Centaures drunken soules to hell,
That under great Alcides furie fell:
And of the dreadfull discord, which did drive
The noble Argonauts to outrage fell,
That each of life sought others to deprive,
All mindlesse of the Golden Fleece, which made them strive.

XXIV

And eke of private persons many moe,
That were too long a worke to count them all;
Some of sworne friends, that did their faith forgoe;
Some of borne brethren, prov'd unnaturall;
Some of deare lovers, foes perpetuall:
Witnesse their broken bandes there to be seene,
Their girlonds rent, their bowres despoyled all;
The moniments whereof there byding beene,
As plaine as at the first, when they were fresh and greene.

XXV

Such was her house within; but all without,
The barren ground was full of wicked weedes,
Which she her selfe had sowen all about,
Now growen great, at first of little seedes,
The seedes of evill wordes and factious deedes;
Which, when to ripenesse due they growen arre,
Bring foorth an infinite increase, that breedes
Tumultuous trouble and contentious jarre,
The which most often end in bloudshed and in warre.

XXVI

And those same cursed seedes doe also serve
To her for bread, and yeeld her living food:
For life it is to her, when others sterve
Through mischievous debate and deadly feood,
That she may sucke their life and drinke their blood,
With which she from her childhood had bene fed:
For she at first was borne of hellish brood,

And by infernall furies nourished,
That by her monstrous shape might easily be red.

XXVII
Her face most fowle and filthy was to see,
With squinted eyes contrarie wayes intended,
And loathly mouth, unmeete a mouth to bee,
That nought but gall and venim comprehended,
And wicked wordes that God and man offended:
Her lying tongue was in two parts divided,
And both the parts did speake, and both contended;
And as her tongue, so was her hart discided,
That never thoght one thing, but doubly stil was guided.

XXVIII
Als as she double spake, so heard she double,
With matchlesse eares deformed and distort,
Fild with false rumors and seditious trouble,
Bred in assemblies of the vulgar sort,
That still are led with every light report.
And as her eares, so eke her feet were odde,
And much unlike, th' one long, the other short,
And both misplast; that, when th' one forward yode,
The other backe retired, and contrarie trode.

XXIX
Likewise unequall were her handes twaine:
That one did reach, the other pusht away;
That one did make, the other mard againe,
And sought to bring all things unto decay;
Whereby great riches, gathered manie a day,
She in short space did often bring to nought,
And their possessours often did dismay:
For all her studie was and all her thought,
How she might overthrow the things that Concord wrought.

XXX
So much her malice did her might surpas,
That even th' Almightie selfe she did maligne,
Because to man so mercifull he was,
And unto all his creatures so benigne,
Sith she her selfe was of his grace indigne:
For all this worlds faire workmanship she tride
Unto his last confusion to bring,
And that great golden chaine quite to divide,
With which it blessed Concord hath together tide.

XXXI
Such was that hag which with Duessa roade,
And serving her in her malitious use,
To hurt good knights, was as it were her baude,

To sell her borrowed beautie to abuse.
For though, like withered tree that wanteth juyce,
She old and crooked were, yet now of late
As fresh and fragrant as the floure deluce
She was become, by chaunge of her estate,
And made full goodly joyance to her new found mate.

XXXII
Her mate, he was a jollie youthfull knight,
That bore great sway in armes and chivalrie,
And was indeed a man of mickle might:
His name was Blandamour, that did descrie
His fickle mind full of inconstancie.
And now himselfe he fitted had right well
With two companions of like qualitie,
Faithlesse Duessa, and false Paridell,
That whether were more false, full hard it is to tell.

XXXIII
Now when this gallant with his goodly crew
From farre espide the famous Britomart,
Like knight adventurous in outward vew,
With his faire paragon, his conquests part,
Approching nigh, eftsoones his wanton hart
Was tickled with delight, and jesting sayd:
'Lo! there, Sir Paridel, for your desart,
Good lucke presents you with yond lovely mayd,
For pitie that ye want a fellow for your ayd.'

XXXIV
By that the lovely paire drew nigh to hond:
Whom when as Paridel more plaine beheld,
Albee in heart he like affection fond,
Yet mindfull how he late by one was feld,
That did those armes and that same scutchion weld,
He had small lust to buy his love so deare,
But answered: 'Sir, him wise I never held,
That, having once escaped perill neare,
Would afterwards afresh the sleeping evill reare.

XXXV
'This knight too late his manhood and his might
I did assay, that me right dearely cost,
Ne list I for revenge provoke new fight,
Ne for light ladies love, that soone is lost.'
The hot-spurre youth so scorning to be crost,
'Take then to you this dame of mine,' quoth hee,
'And I, without your perill or your cost,
Will chalenge yond same other for my fee.'
So forth he fiercely prickt, that one him scarce could see.

XXXVI
The warlike Britonesse her soone addrest,
And with such uncouth welcome did receave
Her fayned paramour, her forced guest,
That, being forst his saddle soone to leave,
Him selfe he did of his new love deceave,
And made him selfe thensample of his follie.
Which done, she passed forth, not taking leave,
And left him now as sad as whilome jollie,
Well warned to beware with whom he dar'd to dallie.

XXXVII
Which when his other companie beheld,
They to his succour ran with readie ayd:
And finding him unable once to weld,
They reared him on horsebacke, and upstayd,
Till on his way they had him forth convayd:
And all the way, with wondrous griefe of mynd
And shame, he shewd him selfe to be dismayd,
More for the love which he had left behynd,
Then that which he had to Sir Paridel resynd.

XXXVIII
Nathlesse he forth did march well as he might,
And made good semblance to his companie,
Dissembling his disease and evill plight;
Till that ere long they chaunced to espie
Two other knights, that towards them did ply
With speedie course, as bent to charge them new.
Whom when as Blandamour approching nie
Perceiv'd to be such as they seemd in vew,
He was full wo, and gan his former griefe renew.

XXXIX
For th' one of them he perfectly descride
To be Sir Scudamour, by that he bore
The God of Love with wings displayed wide,
Whom mortally he hated evermore,
Both for his worth, that all men did adore,
And eke because his love he wonne by right:
Which when he thought, it grieved him full sore,
That, through the bruses of his former fight,
He now unable was to wreake his old despight.

XL
Forthy he thus to Paridel bespake:
'Faire sir, of friendship let me now you pray,
That as I late adventured for your sake,
The hurts whereof me now from battell stay,
Ye will me now with like good turne repay,
And justifie my cause on yonder knight.'

'Ah! sir,' said Paridel, 'do not dismay
Your selfe for this; my selfe will for you fight,
As ye have done for me: the left hand rubs the right.'

XLI
With that he put his spurres unto his steed,
With speare in rest, and toward him did fare,
Like shaft out of a bow preventing speed.
But Scudamour was shortly well aware
Of his approch, and gan him selfe prepare
Him to receive with entertainment meete.
So furiously they met, that either bare
The other downe under their horses feete,
That what of them became themselves did scarsly weete.

XLII
As when two billowes in the Irish sowndes,
Forcibly driven with contrarie tydes,
Do meete together, each abacke rebowndes
With roaring rage; and dashing on all sides,
That filleth all the sea with fome, divydes
The doubtfull current into divers wayes:
So fell those two in spight of both their prydes;
But Scudamour himselfe did soone uprayse,
And mounting light, his foe for lying long upbrayes.

XLIII
Who, rolled on an heape, lay still in swound,
All carelesse of his taunt and bitter rayle;
Till that the rest, him seeing lie on ground,
Ran hastily, to weete what did him ayle:
Where finding that the breath gan him to fayle,
With busie care they strove him to awake,
And doft his helmet, and undid his mayle:
So much they did, that at the last they brake
His slomber, yet so mazed that he nothing spake.

XLIV
Which when as Blandamour beheld, he sayd:
'False faitour Scudamour, that hast by slight
And foule advantage this good knight dismayd,
A knight much better then thy selfe behight,
Well falles it thee that I am not in plight,
This day, to wreake the dammage by thee donne:
Such is thy wont, that still when any knight
Is weakned, then thou doest him overronne:
So hast thou to thy selfe false honour often wonne.'

XLV
He little answer'd, but in manly heart
His mightie indignation did forbeare,

Which was not yet so secret, but some part
Thereof did in his frouning face appeare:
Like as a gloomie cloud, the which doth beare
An hideous storme, is by the northerne blast
Quite overblowne, yet doth not passe so cleare,
But that it all the skie doth overcast
With darknes dred, and threatens all the world to wast.

XLVI
'Ah! gentle knight,' then false Duessa sayd,
'Why do ye strive for ladies love so sore,
Whose chiefe desire is love and friendly aid
Mongst gentle knights to nourish evermore?
Ne be ye wroth, Sir Scudamour, therefore,
That she your love list love another knight,
Ne do your selfe dislike a whit the more;
For love is free, and led with selfe delight,
Ne will enforced be with maisterdome or might.'

XLVII
So false Duessa, but vile Ate thus:
'Both foolish knights, I can but laugh at both,
That strive and storme, with stirre outrageous,
For her that each of you alike doth loth,
And loves another, with whom now she goth
In lovely wise, and sleepes, and sports, and playes;
Whilest both you here with many a cursed oth
Sweare she is yours, and stirre up bloudie frayes,
To win a willow bough, whilest other weares the bayes.'

XLVIII
'Vile hag,' sayd Scudamour, 'why dost thou lye?
And falsly seekst a vertuous wight to shame?'
'Fond knight,' sayd she, 'the thing that with this eye
I saw, why should I doubt to tell the same?'
'Then tell,' quoth Blandamour, 'and feare no blame,
Tell what thou saw'st, maulgre who so it heares.'
'I saw,' quoth she, 'a stranger knight, whose name
I wote not well, but in his shield he beares
(That well I wote) the heads of many broken speares.

XLIX
'I saw him have your Amoret at will,
I saw him kisse, I saw him her embrace,
I saw him sleepe with her all night his fill,
All manie nights, and manie by in place,
That present were to testifie the case.'
Which when as Scudamour did heare, his heart
Was thrild with inward griefe, as when in chace
The Parthian strikes a stag with shivering dart,
The beast astonisht stands in middest of his smart.

L
So stood Sir Scudamour, when this he heard,
Ne word he had to speake for great dismay,
But lookt on Glauce grim, who woxe afeard
Of outrage for the words which she heard say,
Albee untrue she wist them by assay.
But Blandamour, whenas he did espie
His chaunge of cheere, that anguish did bewray,
He woxe full blithe, as he had got thereby,
And gan thereat to triumph without victorie.

LI
'Lo! recreant,' sayd he, 'the fruitlesse end
Of thy vaine boast, and spoile of love misgotten,
Whereby the name of knight-hood thou dost shend,
And all true lovers with dishonor blotten:
All things not rooted well will soone be rotten.'
'Fy, fy! false knight,' then false Duessa cryde,
'Unworthy life, that love with guile hast gotten;
Be thou, where ever thou do go or ryde,
Loathed of ladies all, and of all knights defyde.'

LII
But Scudamour, for passing great despight,
Staid not to answer, scarcely did refraine,
But that in all those knights and ladies sight
He for revenge had guiltlesse Glauce slaine:
But being past, he thus began amaine:
'False traitour squire, false squire of falsest knight,
Why doth mine hand from thine avenge abstaine,
Whose lord hath done my love this foule despight?
Why do I not it wreake on thee now in my might?

LIII
'Discourteous, disloyall Britomart,
Untrue to God, and unto man unjust,
What vengeance due can equall thy desart,
That hast with shamefull spot of sinfull lust
Defil'd the pledge committed to thy trust?
Let ugly shame and endlesse infamy
Colour thy name with foule reproaches rust.
Yet thou, false squire, his fault shalt deare aby,
And with thy punishment his penance shalt supply.'

LIV
The aged dame, him seeing so enraged,
Was dead with feare; nathlesse, as neede required,
His flaming furie sought to have assuaged
With sober words, that sufferance desired
Till time the tryall of her truth expyred:

And evermore sought Britomart to clare.
But he the more with furious rage was fyred,
And thrise his hand to kill her did upreare,
And thrise he drew it backe: so did at last forbeare.

CANTO II

Blandamour winnes false Florimell;
Paridell for her strives;
They are accorded: Agape
Doth lengthen her sonnes lives.

I
Firebrand of hell, first tynd in Phlegeton
By thousand furies, and from thence out throwen
Into this world, to worke confusion
And set it all on fire by force unknowen,
Is wicked discord, whose small sparkes once blowen
None but a god or godlike man can slake;
Such as was Orpheus, that when strife was growen
Amongst those famous ympes of Greece, did take
His silver harpe in hand, and shortly friends them make;

II
Or such as that celestiall Psalmist was,
That when the wicked feend his lord tormented,
With heavenly notes, that did all other pas,
The outrage of his furious fit relented.
Such musicke is wise words with time concented,
To moderate stiffe mindes, disposed to strive:
Such as that prudent Romane well invented,
What time his people into partes did rive,
Them reconcyld againe, and to their homes did drive.

III
Such us'd wise Glauce to that wrathfull knight,
To calme the tempest of his troubled thought:
Yet Blandamour, with termes of foule despight,
And Paridell her scornd, and set at nought,
As old and crooked and not good for ought.
Both they unwise, and warelesse of the evill
That by themselves unto themselves is wrought,
Through that false witch, and that foule aged drevill,
The one a feend, the other an incarnate devill.

IV
With whom as they thus rode accompanide,

They were encountred of a lustie knight,
That had a goodly ladie by his side,
To whom he made great dalliance and delight.
It was to weete the bold Sir Ferraugh hight,
He that from Braggadocchio whilome reft
The snowy Florimell, whose beautie bright
Made him seeme happie for so glorious theft;
Yet was it in due traill but a wandring weft.

V
Which when as Blandamour, whose fancie light
Was alwaies flitting, as the wavering wind,
After each beautie that appeard in sight,
Beheld, eftsoones it prickt his wanton mind
With sting of lust, that reasons eye did blind,
That to Sir Paridell these words he sent:
'Sir knight, why ride ye dumpish thus behind,
Since so good fortune doth to you present
So fayre a spoyle, to make you joyous meriment?'

VI
But Paridell, that had too late a tryall
Of the bad issue of his counsell vaine,
List not to hearke, but made this faire denyall:
'Last turne to hearke, but made this faire denyall:
This now be yours; God send you better gaine.'
Whose scoffed words he taking halfe in scorne,
Fiercely forth prickt his steed, as in disdaine,
Against that knight, ere he him well could torne;
By meanes whereof he hath him lightly overborne.

VII
Who, with the sudden stroke astonisht sore
Upon the ground a while in slomber lay;
The whiles his love away the other bore,
And shewing her, did Paridell upbray:
'Lo! sluggish knight, the victors happie pray!
So Fortune friends the bold:' whom Paridell
Seeing so faire indeede, as he did say,
His hart with secret envie gan to swell,
And inly grudge at him, that he had sped so well.

VIII
Nathlesse proud man himselfe the other deemed,
Having so peerelesse paragon ygot:
For sure the fayrest Florimell him seemed
To him was fallen for his happie lot,
Whose like alive on earth he weened not:
Therefore he her did court, did serve, did wooe,
With humblest suit that he imagine mot,
And all things did devise, and all things dooe,

That might her love prepare, and liking win theretoo.

IX
She, in regard thereof, him recompenst
With golden words and goodly countenance,
And such fond favours sparingly dispenst:
Sometimes him blessing with a light eyeglance,
And coy lookes tempring with loose dalliance;
Sometimes estranging him in sterner wise;
That, having cast him in a foolish trance,
He seemed brought to bed in Paradise,
And prov'd himselfe most foole in what he seem'd most wise.

X
So great a mistresse of her art she was,
And perfectly practiz'd in womans craft,
That though therein himselfe he thought to pas,
And by his false allurements wylie draft
Had thousand women of their love beraft,
Yet now he was surpriz'd: for that false spright,
Which that same witch had in this forme engraft,
Was so expert in every subtile slight,
That it could overreach the wisest earthly wight.

XI
Yet he to her did dayly service more,
And dayly more deceived was thereby;
Yet Paridell him envied therefore,
As seeming plast in sole felicity:
So blind is lust, false colours to descry.
But Ate soone discovering his desire,
And finding now fit opportunity
To stirre up strife twixt love and spight and ire,
Did privily put coles unto his secret fire.

XII
By sundry meanes thereto she prickt him forth,
Now with remembrance of those spightfull speaches,
Now with opinion of his owne more worth,
Now with recounting of like former breaches
Made in their friendship, as that hag him teaches:
And ever when his passion is allayd,
She it revives and new occasion reaches:
That, on a time, as they together way'd,
He made him open chalenge, and thus boldly sayd:

XIII
'Too boastfull Blandamour, too long I beare
The open wrongs thou doest me day by day:
Well know'st thou, when we friendship first did sweare,
The covenant was, that every spoyle or pray

Should equally be shard betwixt us tway:
Where is my part, then, of this ladie bright,
Whom to thy selfe thou takest quite away?
Render therefore therein to me my right,
Or answere for thy wrong, as shall fall out in fight.'

XIV
Exceeding wroth thereat was Blandamour,
And gan this bitter answere to him make:
'Too foolish Paridell, that fayrest floure
Wouldst gather faine, and yet no paines wouldst take!
But not so easie will I her forsake;
This hand her wonne, this hand shall her defend.'
With that they gan their shivering speares to shake,
And deadly points at eithers breast to bend,
Forgetfull each to have bene ever others frend.

XV
Their firie steedes with so untamed forse
Did beare them both to fell avenges end,
That both their speares, with pitilesse remorse,
Through shield and mayle and haberjeon did wend,
And in their flesh a griesly passage rend,
That with the furie of their owne affret
Each other, horse and man, to ground did send;
Where lying still awhile, both did forget
The perilous present stownd in which their lives were set.

XVI
As when two warlike brigandines at sea,
With murdrous weapons arm'd to cruell fight,
Doe meete together on the watry lea,
They stemme ech other with so fell despight,
That with the shocke of their owne heed-lesse might,
Their wooden ribs are shaken nigh a sonder;
They which from shore behold the dreadfull sight
Of flashing fire, and heare the ordenance thonder,
Do greatly stand amaz'd at such unwonted wonder.

XVII
At length they both upstarted in amaze,
As men awaked rashly out of dreme,
And round about themselves a while did gaze;
Till, seeing her that Florimell did seme,
In doubt to whom she victorie should deeme,
Therewith their dulled sprights they edgd anew,
And drawing both their swords with rage extreme,
Like two mad mastiffes each on other flew,
And shields did share, and mailes did rash, and helmes did hew.

XVIII

So furiously each other did assayle,
As if their soules they would attonce have rent
Out of their brests, that streames of bloud did rayle
Adowne, as if their springs of life were spent;
That all the ground with purple bloud was sprent,
And all their armours staynd with bloudie gore;
Yet scarcely once to breath would they relent,
So mortall was their malice and so sore
Become of fayned friendship which they vow'd afore.

XIX
And that which is for ladies most besitting,
To stint all strife, and foster friendly peace,
Was from those dames so farre and so unfitting,
As that, in stead of praying them surcease,
They did much more their cruelty encrease;
Bidding them fight for honour of their love,
And rather die then ladies cause release.
With which vaine termes so much they did them move,
That both resolv'd the last extremities to prove.

XX
There they, I weene, would fight untill this day,
Had not a squire, even he the Squire of Dames,
By great adventure travelled that way;
Who seeing both bent to so bloudy games,
And both of old well knowing by their names,
Drew nigh, to weete the cause of their debate:
And first laide on those ladies thousand blames,
That did not seeke t' appease their deadly hate,
But gazed on their harmes, not pittying their estate.

XXI
And then those knights he humbly did beseech
To stay their hands, till he a while had spoken:
Who lookt a little up at that his speech,
Yet would not let their battell so be broken,
Both greedie fiers on other to be wroken.
Yet he to them so earnestly did call,
And them conjur'd by some well knowen token,
That they at last their wrothfull hands let fall,
Content to heare him speake, and glad to rest withall.

XXII
First he desir'd their cause of strife to see:
They said, it was for love of Florimell.
'Ah! gentle knights,' quoth he, 'how may that bee,
And she so farre astray, as none can tell?'
'Fond squire,' full angry then sayd Paridell,
'Seest not the ladie there before thy face?'
He looked backe, and her advizing well,

Weend, as he said, by that her outward grace,
That fayrest Florimell was present there in place.

XXIII
Glad man was he to see that joyous sight,
For none alive but joy'd in Florimell,
And lowly to her lowting, thus behight:
'Fayrest of faire, that fairenesse doest excell,
This happie day I have to greete you well,
In which you safe I see, whom thousand late
Misdoubted lost through mischiefe that befell;
Long may you live in health and happie state.'
She litle answer'd him, but lightly did aggrate.

XXIV
Then turning to those knights, he gan a new:
'And you, Sir Blandamour and Paridell,
That for this ladie present in your vew
Have rays'd this cruell warre and outrage fell,
Certes, me seemes, bene not advised well,
But rather ought in friendship for her sake
To joyne your force, their forces to repell
That seeke perforce her from you both to take,
And of your gotten spoyle their owne triumph to make.'

XXV
Thereat Sir Blandamour, with countenance sterne,
All full of wrath, thus fiercely him bespake:
'A read, thou squire, that I the man may learne,
That dare fro me thinke Florimell to take.'
'Not one,' quoth he, 'but many doe partake
Herein, as thus: It lately so befell,
That Satyran a girdle did uptake
Well knowne to appertaine to Florimell,
Which for her sake he wore, as him beseemed well.

XXVI
'But when as she her selfe was lost and gone,
Full many knights, that loved her like deare,
Thereat did greatly grudge, that he alone
That lost faire ladies ornament should weare,
And gan therefore close spight to him to beare:
Which he to shun, and stop vile envies sting,
Hath lately caus'd to be proclaim'd each where
A solemne feast, with publike turneying,
To which all knights with them their ladies are to bring.

XXVII
'And of them all she that is fayrest found
Shall have that golden girdle for reward,
And of those knights who is most stout on ground

Shall to that fairest ladie be prefard.
Since therefore she her selfe is now your ward,
To you that ornament of hers pertaines
Against all those that chalenge it to gard,
And save her honour with your ventrous paines;
That shall you win more glory then ye here find gaines.'

XXVIII
When they the reason of his words had hard,
They gan abate the rancour of their rage,
And with their honours and their loves regard
The furious flames of malice to asswage.
Tho each to other did his faith engage,
Like faithfull friends thenceforth to joyne in one
With all their force, and battell strong to wage
Gainst all those knights, as their professed fone,
That chaleng'd ought in Florimell, save they alone.

XXIX
So well accorded forth they rode together
In friendly sort, that lasted but a while,
And of all old dislikes they made faire weather;
Yet all was forg'd and spred with golden foyle;
That under it hidde hate and hollow guyle.
Ne certes can that friendship long endure,
How ever gay and goodly be the style,
That doth ill cause or evill end enure:
For vertue is the band that bindeth harts most sure.

XXX
Thus as they marched all in close disguise
Of fayned love, they chaunst to overtake
Two knights, that lincked rode in lovely wise,
As if they secret counsels did partake;
And each not farre behinde him had his make,
To weete, two ladies of most goodly hew,
That twixt themselves did gentle purpose make,
Unmindfull both of that discordfull crew,
The which with speedie pace did after them pursew.

XXXI
Who, as they now approched nigh at hand,
Deeming them doughtie as they did appeare,
They sent that squire afore, to understand
What mote they be: who, viewing them more neare,
Returned readie newes, that those same weare
Two of the prowest knights in Faery Lond,
And those two ladies their two lovers deare;
Couragious Cambell, and stout Triamond,
With Canacee and Cambine linckt in lovely bond.

XXXII
Whylome, as antique stories tellen us,
Those two were foes the fellonest on ground,
And battell made the dreddest daungerous
That ever shrilling trumpet did resound;
Though now their acts be no where to be found,
As that renowmed poet them compyled
With warlike numbers and heroicke sound,
Dan Chaucer, well of English undefyled,
On Fames eternall beadroll worthie to be fyled.

XXXIII
But wicked Time, that all good thoughts doth waste,
And workes of noblest wits to nought out weare,
That famous moniment hath quite defaste,
And robd the world of threasure endlesse deare,
The which mote have enriched all us heare.
O cursed Eld, the cankerworme of writs!
How may these rimes, so rude as doth appeare,
Hope to endure, sith workes of heavenly wits
Are quite devourd, and brought to nought by little bits?

XXXIV
Then pardon, O most sacred happie spirit,
That I thy labours lost may thus revive,
And steale from thee the meede of thy due merit,
That none durst ever whilest thou wast alive,
And, being dead, in vaine yet many strive:
Ne dare I like, but through infusion sweete
Of thine owne spirit, which doth in me survive,
I follow here the footing of thy feete,
That with thy meaning so I may the rather meete.

XXXV
Cambelloes sister was fayre Canacee,
That was the learnedst ladie in her dayes,
Well seene in everie science that mote bee,
And every secret worke of Natures wayes,
In wittie riddles, and in wise soothsayes,
In power of herbes, and tunes of beasts and burds;
And, that augmented all her other prayse,
She modest was in all her deedes and words,
And wondrous chast of life, yet lov'd of knights and lords.

XXXVI
Full many lords and many knights her loved,
Yet she to none of them her liking lent,
Ne ever was with fond affection moved,
But rul'd her thoughts with goodly governement,
For dread of blame and honours blemishment;
And eke unto her lookes a law she made,

That none of them once out of order went,
But, like to warie centonels well stayd,
Still watcht on every side, of secret foes affrayd.

XXXVII
So much the more as she refusd to love,
So much the more she loved was and sought,
That oftentimes unquiet strife did move
Amongst her lovers, and great quarrels wrought,
That oft for her in bloudie armes they fought.
Which whenas Cambell, that was stout and wise,
Perceiv'd would breede great mischiefe, he bethought
How to prevent the perill that mote rise,
And turne both him and her to honour in this wise.

XXXVIII
One day, when all that troupe of warlike wooers
Assembled were, to weet whose she should bee,
All mightie men and dreadfull derring dooers,
(The harder it to make them well agree)
Amongst them all this end he did decree;
That of them all, which love to her did make,
They by consent should chose the stoutest three,
That with himselfe should combat for her sake,
And of them all the victour should his sister take.

XXXIX
Bold was the chalenge, as himselfe was bold,
And courage full of haughtie hardiment,
Approved oft in perils manifold,
Which he atchiev'd to his great ornament:
But yet his sisters skill unto him lent
Most confidence and hope of happie speed,
Conceived by a ring which she him sent,
That, mongst the manie vertues which we reed,
Had power to staunch al wounds that mortally did bleed.

XL
Well was that rings great vertue knowen to all,
That dread thereof, and his redoubted might,
Did all that youthly rout so much appall,
That none of them durst undertake the fight;
More wise they weend to make of love delight,
Then life to hazard for faire ladies looke,
And yet uncertaine by such outward sight,
Though for her sake they all that perill tooke,
Whether she would them love, or in her liking brooke.

XLI
Amongst those knights there were three brethren bold,
Three bolder brethren never were yborne,

Borne of one mother in one happie mold,
Borne at one burden in one happie morne;
Thrise happie mother, and thrise happie morne,
That bore three such, three such not to be fond!
Her name was Agape, whose children werne
All three as one; the first hight Priamond,
The second Dyamond, the youngest Triamond.

XLII
Stout Priamond, but not so strong to strike,
Strong Diamond, but not so stout a knight,
But Triamond was stout and strong alike:
On horsebacke used Triamond to fight,
And Priamond on foote had more delight,
But horse and foote knew Diamond to wield:
With curtaxe used Diamond to smite,
And Triamond to handle speare and shield,
But speare and curtaxe both usd Priamond in field.

XLIII
These three did love each other dearely well,
And with so firme affection were allyde,
As if but one soule in them all did dwell,
Which did her powre into three parts divyde;
Like three faire branches budding farre and wide,
That from one roote deriv'd their vitall sap:
And like that roote that doth her life divide
Their mother was, and had full blessed hap,
These three so noble babes to bring forth at one clap.

XLIV
Their mother was a Fay, and had the skill
Of secret things, and all the powres of nature,
Which she by art could use unto her will,
And to her service bind each living creature,
Through secret understanding of their feature.
Thereto she was right faire, when so her face
She list discover, and of goodly stature;
But she, as Fayes are wont, in privie place
Did spend her dayes, and lov'd in forests wyld to space.

XLV
There on a day a noble youthly knight,
Seeking adventures in the salvage wood,
Did by great fortune get of her the sight,
As she sate carelesse by a cristall flood,
Combing her golden lockes, as seemd her good;
And unawares upon her laying hold,
That strove in vaine him long to have withstood,
Oppressed her, and there (as it is told)
Got these three lovely babes, that prov'd three champions bold.

XLVI
Which she with her long fostred in that wood,
Till that to ripenesse of mans state they grew:
Then, shewing forth signes of their fathers blood,
They loved armes, and knighthood did ensew,
Seeking adventures, where they anie knew.
Which when their mother saw, she gan to dout
Their safetie, least by searching daungers new,
And rash provoking perils all about,
Their days mote be abridged through their corage stout.

XLVII
Therefore desirous th' end of all their dayes
To know, and them t' enlarge with long extent,
By wondrous skill and many hidden wayes
To the three Fatall Sisters house she went.
Farre under ground from tract of living went,
Downe in the bottome of the deepe Abysse,
Where Demogorgon, in dull darknesse pent,
Farre from the view of gods and heavens blis,
The hideous Chaos keepes, their dreadfull dwelling is.

XLVIII
There she them found, all sitting round about
The direfull distaffe standing in the mid,
And with unwearied fingers drawing out
The lines of life, from living knowledge hid.
Sad Clotho held the rocke, the whiles the thrid
By griesly Lachesis was spun with paine,
That cruell Atropos eftsoones undid,
With cursed knife cutting the twist in twaine:
Most wretched men, whose dayes depend on thrids so vaine!

XLIX
She them saluting, there by them sate still,
Beholding how the thrids of life they span:
And when at last she had beheld her fill,
Trembling in heart, and looking pale and wan,
Her cause of comming she to tell began.
To whom fierce Atropos: 'Bold Fay, that durst
Come see the secret of the life of man,
Well worthie thou to be of Jove accurst,
And eke thy childrens thrids to be a sunder burst.'

L
Whereat she sore affrayd, yet her besought
To graunt her boone, and rigour to abate,
That she might see her childrens thrids forth brought,
And know the measure of their utmost date,
To them ordained by eternall Fate:

Which Clotho graunting, shewed her the same:
That when she saw, it did her much amate
To see their thrids so thin as spiders frame,
And eke so short, that seemd their ends out shortly came.

LI
She then began them humbly to intreate
To draw them longer out, and better twine,
That so their lives might be prolonged late.
But Lachesis thereat gan to repine,
And sayd: 'Fond dame! that deem'st of things divine
As of humane, that they may altred bee,
And chaung'd at pleasure for those impes of thine:
Not so; for what the Fates do once decree,
Not all the gods can chaunge, nor Jove him self can free.'

LII
'Then since,' quoth she, 'the terme of each mans life
For nought may lessened nor enlarged bee,
Graunt this, that when ye shred with fatall knife
His line which is the eldest of the three,
Which is of them the shortest, as I see,
Eftsoones his life may passe into the next;
And when the next shall likewise ended bee,
That both their lives may likewise be annext
Unto the third, that his may so be trebly wext.'

LIII
They graunted it; and then that carefull Fay
Departed thence with full contented mynd;
And comming home, in warlike fresh aray
Them found all three, according to their kynd:
But unto them what destinie was assynd,
Or how their lives were eekt, she did not tell;
But evermore, when she fit time could fynd,
She warned them to tend their safeties well,
And love each other deare, what ever them befell.

LIV
So did they surely during all their dayes,
And never discord did amongst them fall;
Which much augmented all their other praise.
And now, t' increase affection naturall,
In love of Canacee they joyned all:
Upon which ground this same great battell grew,
Great matter growing of beginning small;
The which, for length, I will not here pursew,
But rather will reserve it for a canto new.

CANTO III

The battell twixt three brethren with
Cambell for Canacee:
Cambina with true friendships bond
Doth their long strife agree.

I
O why doe wretched men so much desire
To draw their dayes unto the utmost date,
And doe not rather wish them soone expire,
Knowing the miserie of their estate,
And thousand perills which them still awate,
Tossing them like a boate amid the mayne,
That every houre they knocke at Deathes gate?
And he that happie seemes and least in payne,
Yet is as nigh his end as he that most doth playne.

II
Therefore this Fay I hold but fond and vaine,
The which, in seeking for her children three
Long life, thereby did more prolong their paine.
Yet whilest they lived none did ever see
More happie creatures then they seem'd to bee,
Nor more ennobled for their courtesie,
That made them dearely lov'd of each degree,
Ne more renowmed for their chevalrie,
That made them dreaded much of all men farre and nie.

III
These three that hardie chalenge tooke in hand,
For Canacee with Cambell for to fight:
The day was set, that all might understand,
And pledges pawnd the same to keepe a right:
That day, the dreddest day that living wight
Did ever see upon this world to shine,
So soone as heavens window shewed light,
These warlike champions, all in armour shine,
Assembled were in field, the chalenge to define.

IV
The field with listes was all about enclos'd,
To barre the prease of people farre away;
And at th' one side sixe judges were dispos'd,
To view and deeme the deedes of armes that day;
And on the other side, in fresh aray,
Fayre Canacee upon a stately stage
Was set, to see the fortune of that fray,
And to be seene, as his most worthie wage

That could her purchase with his lives adventur'd gage.

V

Then entred Cambell first into the list,
With stately steps and fearelesse countenance,
As if the conquest his he surely wist.
Soone after did the brethren three advance,
In brave aray and goodly amenance,
With scutchins gilt and banners broad displayd;
And marching thrise in warlike ordinance,
Thrise lowted lowly to the noble mayd,
The whiles shril trompets and loud clarions sweetly playd.

VI

Which doen, the doughty chalenger came forth,
All arm'd to point, his chalenge to abet:
Gainst whom Sir Priamond, with equall worth
And equall armes, himselfe did forward set.
A trompet blew; they both together met
With dreadfull force and furious intent,
Carelesse of perill in their fiers affret,
As if that life to losse they had forelent,
And cared not to spare that should be shortly spent.

VII

Right practicke was Sir Priamond in fight,
And throughly skild in use of shield and speare;
Ne lesse approved was Cambelloes might,
Ne lesse his skill in weapons did appeare,
That hard it was to weene which harder were.
Full many mightie strokes on either side
Were sent, that seemed death in them to beare,
But they were both so watchfull and well eyde,
That they avoyded were, and vainely by did slyde.

VIII

Yet one of many was so strongly bent
By Priamond, that with unluckie glaunce
Through Cambels shoulder it unwarely went,
That forced him his shield to disadvaunce:
Much was he grieved with that gracelesse chaunce,
Yet from the wound no drop of bloud there fell,
But wondrous paine, that did the more enhaunce
His haughtie courage to advengement fell:
Smart daunts not mighty harts, but makes them more to swell.

IX

With that, his poynant speare he fierce aventred,
With doubled force, close underneath his shield,
That through the mayles into his thigh it entred,
And there arresting, readie way did yield

For bloud to gush forth on the grassie field;
That he for paine himselfe not right upreare,
But too and fro in great amazement reel'd,
Like an old oke, whose pith and sap is seare,
At puffe of every storme doth stagger here and there.

X
Whom so dismayd when Cambell had espide,
Againe he drove at him with double might,
That nought mote stay the steele, till in his side
The mortall point most cruelly empight:
Where fast infixed, whilest he sought by slight
It forth to wrest, the staffe a sunder brake,
And left the head behind: with which despight
He all enrag'd, his shivering speare did shake,
And charging him a fresh, thus felly him bespake:

XI
'Lo! faitour, there thy meede unto thee take,
The meede of thy mischalenge and abet:
Not for thine owne, but for thy sisters sake,
Have I thus long thy life unto thee let:
But to forbeare doth not forgive the det.'
The wicked weapon heard his wrathfull vow,
And passing forth with furious affret,
Pierst through his bever quite into his brow,
That with the force it backward forced him to bow.

XII
Therewith a sunder in the midst it brast,
And in his hand nought but the troncheon left;
The other halfe behind yet sticking fast
Out of his headpeece Cambell fiercely reft,
And with such furie backe at him it heft,
That, making way unto his dearest life,
His weasand pipe it through his gorget cleft:
Thence streames of purple bloud issuing rife
Let forth his wearie ghost, and made an end of strife.

XIII
His wearie ghost, assoyld from fleshly band,
Did not, as others wont, directly fly
Unto her rest in Plutoes griesly land,
Ne into ayre did vanish presently,
Ne chaunged was into a starre in sky:
But through traduction was eftsoones derived,
Like as his mother prayd the Destinie,
Into his other brethren that survived,
In whom he liv'd a new, of former life deprived.

XIV

Whom when on ground his brother next beheld,
Though sad and sorie for so heavy sight,
Yet leave unto his sorrow did not yeeld;
But rather stird to vengeance and despight,
Through secret feeling of his generous spright,
Rusht fiercely forth, the battell to renew,
As in reversion of his brothers right;
And chalenging the virgin as his dew.
His foe was soone addrest: the trompets freshly blew.

XV
With that they both together fiercely met,
As if that each ment other to devoure;
And with their axes both so sorely bet,
That neither plate nor mayle, whereas their powre
They felt, could once sustaine the hideous stowre,
But rived were like rotten wood a sunder,
Whilest through their rifts the ruddie bloud did showre,
And fire did flash, like lightning after thunder,
That fild the lookers on attonce with ruth and wonder.

XVI
As when two tygers, prickt with hungers rage,
Have by good fortune found some beasts fresh spoyle,
On which they weene their famine to asswage,
And gaine a feastfull guerdon of their toyle;
Both falling out doe stirre up strifefull broyle,
And cruell battell twixt themselves doe make,
Whiles neither lets the other touch the soyle,
But either sdeignes with other to partake:
So cruelly these knights strove for that ladies sake.

XVII
Full many strokes, that mortally were ment,
The whiles were enterchaunged twixt them two;
Yet they were all with so good wariment
Or warded, or avoyded and let goe,
That still the life stood fearelesse of her foe:
Till Diamond, disdeigning long delay
Of doubtfull fortune wavering to and fro,
Resolv'd to end it one or other way;
And heav'd his murdrous axe at him with mighty sway.

XVIII
The dreadfull stroke, in case it had arrived
Where it was ment, (so deadly it was ment)
The soule had sure out of his bodie rived,
And stinted all the strife incontinent.
But Cambels fate that fortune did prevent:
For seeing it at hand, he swarv'd asyde,
And so gave way unto his fell intent:

Who, missing of the marke which he had eyde,
Was with the force nigh feld whilst his right foot did slyde.

XIX
As when a vulture greedie of his pray,
Through hunger long, that hart to him doth lend,
Strikes at an heron with all his bodies sway,
That from his force seemes nought may it defend;
The warie fowle, that spies him toward bend
His dreadfull souse, avoydes it, shunning light,
And maketh him his wing in vaine to spend;
That with the weight of his owne weeldlesse might,
He falleth nigh to ground, and scarse recovereth flight.

XX
Which faire adventure when Cambello spide,
Full lightly, ere himselfe he could recower,
From daungers dread to ward his naked side,
He can let drive at him with all his power,
And with his axe him smote in evill hower,
That from his shoulders quite his head he reft:
The headlesse tronke, as heedlesse of that stower,
Stood still a while, and his fast footing kept,
Till, feeling life to fayle, it fell, and deadly slept.

XXI
They which that piteous spectacle beheld
Were much amaz'd the headlesse tronke to see
Stand up so long, and weapon vaine to weld,
Unweeting of the Fates divine decree
For lifes succession in those brethren three.
For notwithstanding that one soule was reft,
Yet, had the bodie not dismembred bee,
It would have lived, and revived eft;
But finding no fit seat, the lifelesse corse it left.

XXII
It left; but that same soule which therein dwelt,
Streight entring into Triamond, him fild
With double life and griefe; which when he felt,
As one whose inner parts had bene ythrild
With point of steele, that close his hartbloud spild,
He lightly lept out of his place of rest,
And rushing forth into the emptie field,
Against Cambello fiercely him addrest;
Who him affronting soone to fight was readie prest.

XXIII
Well mote ye wonder how that noble knight,
After he had so often wounded beene,
Could stand on foot now to renew the fight.

But had ye then him forth advauncing seene,
Some newborne wight ye would him surely weene,
So fresh he seemed and so fierce in sight;
Like as a snake, whom wearie winters teene
Hath worne to nought, now feeling sommers might,
Casts off his ragged skin and freshly doth him dight.

XXIV
All was through vertue of the ring he wore,
The which not onely did not from him let
One drop of bloud to fall, but did restore
His weakned powers, and dulled spirits whet,
Through working of the stone therein yset.
Else how could one of equall might with most,
Against so many no lesse mightie met,
Once thinke to match three such on equall cost,
Three such as able were to match a puissant host?

XXV
Yet nought thereof was Triamond adredde,
Ne desperate of glorious victorie,
But sharpely him assayld, and sore bestedde,
With heapes of strokes, which he at him let flie
As thicke as hayle forth poured from the skie:
He stroke, he soust, he foynd, he hewd, he lasht,
And did his yron brond so fast applie,
That from the same the fierie sparkles flasht,
As fast as water-sprinkles gainst a rocke are dasht.

XXVI
Much was Cambello daunted with his blowes,
So thicke they fell, and forcibly were sent,
That he was forst from daunger of the throwes
Backe to retire, and somewhat to relent,
Till th' heat of his fierce furie he had spent:
Which when for want of breath gan to abate,
He then afresh with new encouragement
Did him assayle, and mightily amate,
As fast as forward erst, now backward to retrate.

XXVII
Like as the tide, that comes fro th' ocean mayne,
Flowes up the Shenan with contrarie forse,
And overruling him in his owne rayne,
Drives backe the current of his kindly course,
And makes it seeme to have some other sourse:
But when the floud is spent, then backe againe,
His borrowed waters forst to redisbourse,
He sends the sea his owne with double gaine,
And tribute eke withall, as to his soveraine.

XXVIII
Thus did the battell varie to and fro,
With diverse fortune doubtfull to be deemed:
Now this the better had, now had his fo;
Then he halfe vanquisht, then the other seemed;
Yet victors both them selves alwayes esteemed.
And all the while the disentrayled blood
Adowne their sides like litle rivers stremed,
That with the wasting of his vitall flood
Sir Triamond at last full faint and feeble stood.

XXIX
But Cambell still more strong and greater grew,
Ne felt his blood to wast, ne powres emperisht,
Through that rings vertue, that with vigour new,
Still when as he enfeebled was, him cherisht,
And all his wounds and all his bruses guarisht:
Like as a withered tree, through husbands toyle,
Is often seene full freshly to have florisht,
And fruitfull seene full freshly to have florisht,
As fresh as when it first was planted in the soyle.

XXX
Through which advantage, in his strength he rose,
And smote the other with so wondrous might,
That through the seame which did his hauberk close
Into his throate and life it pierced quight,
That downe he fell as dead in all mens sight:
Yet dead he was not, yet he sure did die,
As all men do that lose the living spright:
So did one soule out of his bodie flie
Unto her native home from mortall miserie.

XXXI
But nathelesse whilst all the lookers on
Him dead behight, as he to all appeard,
All unawares he started up anon,
As one that had out of a dreame bene reard,
And fresh assayld his foe; who halfe affeard
Of th' uncouth sight, as he some ghost had seene,
Stood still amaz'd, holding his idle sweard;
Till, having often by him stricken beene,
He forced was to strike, and save him selfe from teene.

XXXII
Yet from thenceforth more warily he fought,
As one in feare the Stygian gods t' offend,
Ne followd on so fast, but rather sought
Him selfe to save, and daunger to defend,
Then life and labour both in vaine to spend.
Which Triamond perceiving, weened sure

He gan to faint toward the battels end,
And that he should not long on foote endure,
A signe which did to him the victorie assure.

XXXIII
Whereof full blith, eftsoones his mightie hand
He heav'd on high, in mind with that same blow
To make an end of all that did withstand:
Which Cambell seeing come, was nothing slow
Him selfe to save from that so deadly throw;
And at that instant reaching forth his sweard,
Close underneath his shield, that scarce did show,
Stroke him, as he his hand to strike upreard,
In th' arm-pit full, that through both sides the wound appeard.

XXXIV
Yet still that direfull stroke kept on his way,
And falling heavie on Cambelloes crest,
Strooke him so hugely that in swowne he lay,
And in his head an hideous wound imprest:
And sure, had it not happily found rest
Upon the brim of his brode plated shield,
It would have cleft his braine downe to his brest.
So both at once fell dead upon the field,
And each to other seemd the victorie to yield.

XXXV
Which when as all the lookers on beheld,
They weened sure the warre was at an end,
And judges rose, and marshals of the field
Broke up the listes, their armes away to rend;
And Canacee gan wayle her dearest frend.
All suddenly they both upstarted light,
The one out of the swownd which him did blend,
The other breathing now another spright,
And fiercely each assayling, gan afresh to fight.

XXXVI
Long while they then continued in that wize,
As if but then the battell had begonne:
Strokes, wounds, wards, weapons, all they did despise,
Ne either car'd to ward, or perill shonne,
Desirous both to have the battell donne;
Ne either cared life to save or spill,
Ne which of them did winne, ne which were wonne.
So wearie both of fighting had their fill,
That life it selfe seemd loathsome, and long safetie ill.

XXXVII
Whilst thus the case in doubtfull ballance hong,
Unsure to whether side it would incline,

And all mens eyes and hearts, which there among
Stood gazing, filled were with rufull tine,
And secret feare to see their fatall fine,
All suddenly they heard a troublous noyes,
That seemd some perilous tumult to desine,
Confusd with womens cries and shouts of boyes,
Such as the troubled theaters oftimes annoyes.

XXXVIII
Thereat the champions both stood still a space,
To weeten what that sudden clamour ment;
Lo! where they spyde with speedie whirling pace
One in a charet of straunge furniment
Towards them driving like a storme out sent.
The charet decked was in wondrous wize
With gold and many a gorgeous ornament,
After the Persian Monarks antique guize,
Such as the maker selfe could best by art devize.

XXXIX
And drawne it was (that wonder is to tell)
Of two grim lyons, taken from the wood,
In which their powre all others did excell;
Now made forget their former cruell mood,
T' obey their riders hest, as seemed good.
And therein sate a ladie passing faire
And bright, that seemed borne of angels brood,
And with her beautie bountie did compare,
Whether of them in her should have the greater share.

XL
Thereto she learned was in magicke leare,
And all the artes that subtill wits discover,
Having therein bene trained many a yeare,
And well instructed by the Fay her mother,
That in the same she farre exceld all other.
Who, understanding by her mightie art
Of th' evill plight in which her dearest brother
Now stood, came forth in hast to take his part,
And pacifie the strife which causd so deadly smart.

XLI
And as she passed through th' unruly preace
Of people thronging thicke her to behold,
Her angrie teame, breaking their bonds of peace,
Great heapes of them, like sheepe in narrow fold,
For hast did over-runne, in dust enrould;
That, thorough rude confusion of the rout,
Some fearing shriekt, some being harmed hould,
Some laught for sport, some did for wonder shout,
And some, that would seeme wise, their wonder turnd to dout.

XLII
In her right hand a rod of peace shee bore,
About the which two serpents weren wound,
Entrayled mutually in lovely lore,
And by the tailes together firmely bound,
And both were with one olive garland crownd,
Like to the rod which Maias sonne doth wield,
Wherewith the hellish fiends he doth confound.
And in her other hand a cup she hild,
The which was with Nepenthe to the brim upfild.

XLIII
Nepenthe is a drinck of soverayne grace,
Devized by the gods, for to asswage
Harts grief, and bitter gall away to chace,
Which stirs up anguish and contentious rage:
In stead thereof sweet peace and quietage
It doth establish in the troubled mynd.
Few men, but such as sober are and sage,
Are by the gods to drinck thereof assynd;
But such as drinck, eternall happinesse do fynd.

XLIV
Such famous men, such worthies of the earth,
As Jove will have advaunced to the skie,
And there made gods, though borne of mortall berth,
For their high merits and great dignitie,
Are wont, before they may to heaven flie,
To drincke hereof, whereby all cares forepast
Are washt away quite from their memorie.
So did those olde heroes hereof taste,
Before that they in blisse amongst the gods were plaste.

XLV
Much more of price and of more gratious powre
Is this, then that same water of Ardenne,
The which Rinaldo drunck in happie howre,
Described by that famous Tuscane penne:
For that had might to change the hearts of men
Fro love to hate, a change of evill choise:
But this doth hatred make in love to brenne,
And heavy heart with comfort doth rejoyce.
Who would not to this vertue rather yeeld his voice?

XLVI
At last arriving by the listes side,
Shee with her rod did softly smite the raile,
Which straight flew ope, and gave her way to ride.
Eftsoones out of her coch she gan availe,
And pacing fairely forth, did bid all haile,

First to her brother, whom she loved deare,
That so to see him made her heart to quaile:
And next to Cambell, whose sad ruefull cheare
Made her to change her hew, and hidden love t' appeare.

XLVII
They lightly her requit (for small delight
They had as then her long to entertaine,)
And eft them turned both againe to fight:
Which when she saw, downe on the bloudy plaine
Her selfe she threw, and teares gan shed amaine;
Amongst her teares immixing prayers meeke,
And with her prayers reasons, to restraine
From blouddy strife; and blessed peace to seeke,
By all that unto them was deare, did them beseeke.

XLVIII
But when as all might nought with them prevaile,
Shee smote them lightly with her powrefull wand.
Then suddenly as if their hearts did faile,
Their wrathfull blades downe fell out of their hand,
And they like men astonisht still did stand.
Thus whilest their minds were doubtfully distraught,
And mighty spirites bound with mightier band,
Her golden cup to them for drinke she raught,
Whereof, full glad for thirst, ech drunk an harty draught.

XLIX
Of which so soone as they once tasted had,
Wonder it is that sudden change to see:
Instead of strokes, each other kissed glad,
And lovely haulst, from feare of treason free,
And plighted hands for ever friends to be.
When all men saw this sudden change of things,
So mortall foes so friendly to agree,
For passing joy, which so great marvaile brings,
They all gan shout aloud, that all the heaven rings.

L
All which when gentle Canacee beheld,
In hast she from her lofty chaire descended,
Too weet what sudden tidings was befeld:
Where when she saw that cruell war so ended,
And deadly foes so faithfully affrended,
In lovely wise she gan that lady greet,
Which had so great dismay so well amended,
And entertaining her with curt'sies meet,
Profest to her true friendship and affection sweet.

LI
Thus when they all accorded goodly were,

The trumpets sounded, and they all arose,
Thence to depart with glee and gladsome chere.
Those warlike champions both together chose
Homeward to march, themselves there to repose,
And wise Cambina, taking by her side
Faire Canacee, as fresh as morning rose,
Unto her coch remounting, home did ride,
Admir'd of all the people and much glorifide.

LII
Where making joyous feast theire daies they spent
In perfect love, devoide of hatefull strife,
Allide with bands of mutuall couplement;
For Triamond had Canacee to wife,
With whom he ledd a long and happie life;
And Cambel tooke Cambina to his fere,
The which as life were each to other liefe.
So all alike did love, and loved were,
That since their days such lovers were not found elswhere.

CANTO IV

Satyrane makes a turneyment
For love of Florimell:
Britomart winnes the prize from all,
And Artegall doth quell.

I
It often fals, (as here it earst befell)
That mortall foes doe turne to faithfull frends,
And friends profest are chaungd to foemen fell:
The cause of both, of both their minds depends,
And th' end of both, likewise of both their ends:
For enmitie, that of no ill proceeds,
But of occasion, with th' occasion ends;
And friendship, which a faint affection breeds
Without regard of good, dyes like ill grounded seeds.

II
That well (me seemes) appeares by that of late
Twixt Cambell and Sir Triamond befell,
As els by this, that now a new debate
Stird up twixt Blandamour and Paridell,
The which by course befals me here to tell:
Who having those two other knights espide,
Marching afore, as ye remember well,
Sent forth their squire to have them both descride,

And eke those masked ladies riding them beside.

III
Who backe returning, told as he had seene,
That they were doughtie knights of dreaded name,
And those two ladies their two loves unseene;
And therefore wisht them without blot or blame
To let them passe at will, for dread of shame.
But Blandamour, full of vainglorious spright,
And rather stird by his discordfull dame,
Upon them gladly would have prov'd his might,
But that he yet was sore of his late lucklesse fight.

IV
Yet, nigh approching, he them fowle bespake,
Disgracing them, him selfe thereby to grace,
As was his wont, so weening way to make
To ladies love, where so he came in place,
And with lewd termes their lovers to deface.
Whose sharpe provokement them incenst so sore,
That both were bent t' avenge his usage base,
And gan their shields addresse them selves afore:
For evill deedes may better then bad words be bore.

V
But faire Cambina with perswasions myld
Did mitigate the fiercenesse of their mode,
That for the present they were reconcyld,
And gan to treate of deeds of armes abrode,
And strange adventures, all the way they rode:
Amongst the which they told, as then befell,
Of that great turney which was blazed brode,
For that rich girdle of faire Florimell,
The prize of her which did in beautie most excell.

VI
To which folke-mote they all with one consent,
Sith each of them his ladie had him by,
Whose beautie each of them thought excellent,
Agreed to travell, and their fortunes try.
So as they passed forth, they did espy
One in bright armes, with ready speare in rest,
That toward them his course seem'd to apply;
Gainst whom Sir Paridell himselfe addrest,
Him weening, ere he nigh approcht, to have represt.

VII
Which th' other seeing, gan his course relent,
And vaunted speare eftsoones to disadvaunce,
As if he naught but peace and pleasure ment,
Now falne into their fellowship by chance;

Whereat they shewed curteous countenaunce.
So as he rode with them accompanide,
His roving eie did on the lady glaunce
Which Blandamour had riding by his side:
Whom sure he weend that he some wher tofore had eide.

VIII
It was to weete that snowy Florimell,
Which Ferrau late from Braggadochio wonne;
Whom he now seeing, her remembred well,
How, having reft her from the witches sonne,
He soone her lost: wherefore he now begunne
To challenge her anew, as his owne prize,
Whom formerly he had in battell wonne,
And proffer made by force her to reprize:
Which scornefull offer Blandamour gan soone despize;

IX
And said: 'Sir knight, sith ye this lady clame,
Whom he that hath were loth to lose so light,
(For so to lose a lady were great shame,)
Yee shall her winne, as I have done, in fight:
And lo! shee shall be placed here in sight,
Together with this hag beside her set,
That who so winnes her may her have by right:
But he shall have the hag that is ybet,
And with her alwaies ride, till he another get.'

X
That offer pleased all the company,
So Florimell with Ate forth was brought,
At which they all gan laugh full merrily:
But Braggadochio said, he never thought
For such an hag, that seemed worse then nought,
His person to emperill so in fight:
But if to match that lady they had sought
Another like, that were like faire and bright,
His life he then would spend to justifie his right.

XI
At which his vaine excuse they all gan smile,
As scorning his unmanly cowardize:
And Florimell him fowly gan revile,
That for her sake refus'd to enterprize
The battell, offred in so knightly wize:
And Ate eke provokt him privily
With love of her, and shame of such mesprize.
But naught he car'd for friend or enemy,
For in base mind nor friendship dwels nor enmity.

XII

But Cambell thus did shut up all in jest:
'Brave knights and ladies, certes ye doe wrong
To stirre up strife, when most us needeth rest,
That we may us reserve both fresh and strong
Against the turneiment, which is not long,
When who so list to fight may fight his fill:
Till then your challenges ye may prolong;
And then it shall be tried, if ye will,
Whether shall have the hag, or hold the lady still.'

XIII
They all agreed; so, turning all to game
And pleasaunt bord, they past forth on their way,
And all that while, where so they rode or came,
That masked mock-knight was their sport and play.
Till that at length, upon th' appointed day,
Unto the place of turneyment they came;
Where they before them found in fresh aray
Manie a brave knight and manie a daintie dame
Assembled, for to get the honour of that game.

XIV
There this faire crewe arriving did divide
Them selves asunder: Blandamour with those
Of his on th' one; the rest on th' other side.
But boastfull Braggadocchio rather chose,
For glorie vaine, their fellowship to lose,
That men on him the more might gaze alone.
The rest them selves in troupes did else dispose,
Like as it seemed best to every one;
The knights in couples marcht, with ladies linckt attone.

XV
Then first of all forth came Sir Satyrane,
Bearing that precious relicke in an arke
Of gold, that bad eyes might it not prophane:
Which drawing softly forth out of the darke,
He open shewd, that all men it mote marke.
A gorgeous girdle, curiously embost
With pearle and precious stone, worth many a marke;
Yet did the workmanship farre passe the cost:
It was the same which lately Florimel had lost.

XVI
That same aloft he hong in open vew,
To be the prize of beautie and of might;
The which eftsoones discovered, to it drew
The eyes of all, allur'd with close delight,
And hearts quite robbed with so glorious sight,
That all men threw out vowes and wishes vaine.
Thrise happie ladie, and thrise happie knight,

Them seemd, that could so goodly riches gaine,
So worthie of the perill, worthy of the paine.

XVII
Then tooke the bold Sir Satyrane in hand
An huge great speare, such as he wont to wield,
And vauncing forth from all the other band
Of knights, addrest his maiden-headed shield,
Shewing him selfe all ready for the field.
Gainst whom there singled from the other side
A Painim knight, that well in armes was skild,
And had in many a battell oft bene tride,
Hight Bruncheval the bold, who fiersly forth did ride.

XVIII
So furiously they both together met,
That neither could the others force sustaine:
As two fierce buls, that strive the rule to get
Of all the heard, meete with so hideous maine,
That both, rebutted, tumble on the plaine;
So these two champions to the ground were feld,
Where in a maze they both did long remaine,
And in their hands their idle troncheons held,
Which neither able were to wag, or once to weld.

XIX
Which when the noble Ferramont espide,
He pricked forth in ayd of Satyran;
And him against Sir Blandamour did ride
With all the strength and stifnesse that he can.
But the more strong and stiffely that he ran,
So much more sorely to the ground he fell,
That on an heape were tumbled horse and man.
Unto whose rescue forth rode Paridell;
But him likewise with that same speare he eke did quell.

XX
Which Braggadocchio seeing, had no will
To hasten greatly to his parties ayd,
Albee his turne were next; but stood there still,
As one that seemed doubtfull or dismayd.
But Triamond, halfe wroth to see him staid,
Sternly stept forth, and raught away his speare,
With which so sore he Ferramont assaid,
That horse and man to ground he quite did beare,
That neither could in hast themselves againe upreare.

XXI
Which to avenge, Sir Devon him did dight,
But with no better fortune then the rest,
For him likewise he quickly downe did smight;

And after him Sir Douglas him addrest,
And after him Sir Paliumord forth prest,
But none of them against his strokes could stand;
But all the more, the more his praise increst:
For either they were left uppon the land,
Or went away sore wounded of his haplesse hand.

XXII
And now by this, Sir Satyrane abraid
Out of the swowne, in which too long he lay;
And looking round about, like one dismaid,
When as he saw the mercilesse affray
Which doughty Triamond had wrought that day
Unto the noble Knights of Maidenhead,
His mighty heart did almost rend in tway
For very gall, that rather wholly dead
Himselfe he wisht have beene, then in so bad a stead.

XXIII
Eftsoones he gan to gather up around
His weapons, which lay scattered all abrode,
And as it fell, his steed he ready found.
On whom remounting, fiercely forth he rode,
Like sparke of fire that from the andvile glode,
There where he saw the valiant Triamond
Chasing, and laying on them heavy lode,
That none his force were able to withstond,
So dreadfull were his strokes, so deadly was his hond.

XXIV
With that, at him his beamlike speare he aimed,
And thereto all his power and might applide:
The wicked steele for mischiefe first ordained,
And having now misfortune got for guide,
Staid not till it arrived in his side,
And therein made a very griesly wound,
That streames of bloud his armour all bedide.
Much was he daunted with that direfull stound,
That scarse he him upheld from falling in a sound.

XXV
Yet as he might, himselfe he soft withdrew
Out of the field, that none perceiv'd it plaine.
Then gan the part of chalengers anew
To range the field, and victorlike to raine,
That none against them battell durst maintaine.
By that the gloomy evening on them fell,
That forced them from fighting to refraine,
And trumpets sound to cease did them compell.
So Satyrane that day was judg'd to beare the bell.

XXVI
The morrow next the turney gan anew,
And with the first the hardy Satyrane
Appear'd in place, with all his noble crew:
On th' other side full many a warlike swaine
Assembled were, that glorious prize to gaine.
But mongst them all was not Sir Triamond;
Unable he new battell to darraine,
Through grievaunce of his late received wound,
That doubly did him grieve, when so himselfe he found.

XXVII
Which Cambell seeing, though he could not salve,
Ne done undoe, yet for to salve his name,
And purchase honour in his friends behalve,
This goodly counterfesaunce he did frame:
The shield and armes, well knowne to be the same
Which Triamond had worne, unwares to wight,
And to his friend unwist, for doubt of blame,
If he misdid, he on himselfe did dight,
That none could him discerne, and so went forth to fight.

XXVIII
There Satyrane lord of the field he found,
Triumphing in great joy and jolity;
Gainst whom none able was to stand on ground;
That much he gan his glorie to envy,
And cast t' avenge his friends indignity.
A mightie speare eftsoones at him he bent;
Who, seeing him come on so furiously,
Met him mid-way with equall hardiment,
That forcibly to ground they both together went.

XXIX
They up againe them selves can lightly reare,
And to their tryed swords them selves betake;
With which they wrought such wondrous marvels there,
That all the rest it did amazed make,
Ne any dar'd their perill to partake;
Now cuffing close, now chacing to and fro,
Now hurtling round advantage for to take:
As two wild boares together grapling go,
Chaufing and foming choler each against his fo.

XXX
So as they courst, and turneyd here and theare,
It chaunst Sir Satyrane his steed at last,
Whether through foundring, or through sodein feare,
To stumble, that his rider nigh he cast;
Which vauntage Cambell did pursue so fast,
That ere him selfe he had recovered well,

So sore he sowst him on the compast creast,
That forced him to leave his loftie sell,
And rudely tumbling downe under his horse feete fell.

XXXI
Lightly Cambello leapt downe from his steed,
For to have rent his shield and armes away,
That whylome wont to be the victors meed;
When all unwares he felt an hideous sway
Of many swords, that lode on him did lay.
An hundred knights had him enclosed round,
To rescue Satyrane out of his pray;
All which at once huge strokes on him did pound,
In hope to take him prisoner, where he stood on ground.

XXXII
He with their multitude was nought dismayd,
But with stout courage turnd upon them all,
And with his brondiron round about him layd;
Of which he dealt large almes, as did befall:
Like as a lion, that by chaunce doth fall
Into the hunters toile, doth rage and rore,
In royall heart disdaining to be thrall.
But all in vaine: for what might one do more?
They have him taken captive, though it grieve him sore.

XXXIII
Whereof when newes to Triamond was brought,
There as he lay, his wound he soone forgot,
And starting up, streight for his armour sought:
In vaine he sought; for there he found it not;
Cambello it away before had got:
Cambelloes armes therefore he on him threw,
And lightly issewd forth to take his lot.
There he in troupe found all that warlike crew,
Leading his friend away, full sorie to his vew.

XXXIV
Into the thickest of that knightly preasse
He thrust, and smote downe all that was betweene,
Caried with fervent zeale, ne did he ceasse,
Till that he came where he had Cambell seene,
Like captive thral two other knights atweene:
There he amongst them cruell havocke makes,
That they which lead him soone enforced beene
To let him loose, to save their proper stakes;
Who being freed, from one a weapon fiercely takes.

XXXV
With that he drives at them with dreadfull might,
Both in remembrance of his friends late harme,

And in revengement of his owne despight;
So both together give a new allarme,
As if but now the battell wexed warme.
As when two greedy wolves doe breake by force
Into an heard, farre from the husband farme,
They spoile and ravine without all remorse;
So did these two through all the field their foes enforce.

XXXVI
Fiercely they followd on their bolde emprize,
Till trumpets sound did warne them all to rest;
Then all with one consent did yeeld the prize
To Triamond and Cambell as the best.
But Triamond to Cambell it relest,
And Cambell it to Triamond transferd;
Each labouring t' advance the others gest,
And make his praise before his owne preferd:
So that the doome was to another day differd.

XXXVII
The last day came, when all those knightes againe
Assembled were their deedes of armes to shew.
Full many deedes that day were shewed plaine:
But Satyrane, bove all the other crew,
His wondrous worth declared in all mens view;
For from the first he to the last endured,
And though some while Fortune from him withdrew,
Yet evermore his honour he recured,
And with unwearied powre his party still assured.

XXXVIII
Ne was there knight that ever thought of armes,
But that his utmost prowesse there made knowen;
That by their many wounds, and carelesse harmes,
By shivered speares, and swords all under strowen,
By scattered shields was easie to be showen.
There might ye see loose steeds at randon ronne,
Whose luckelesse riders late were over-throwen,
And squiers make hast to helpe their lords fordonne:
But still the Knights of Maidenhead the better wonne.

XXXIX
Till that there entred on the other side
A straunger knight, from whence no man could reed,
In queynt disguise, full hard to be descride.
For all his armour was like salvage weed,
With woody mosse bedight, and all his steed
With oaken leaves attrapt, that seemed fit
For salvage wight, and thereto well agreed
His word, which on his ragged shield was writ,
Salvagesse sans finesse, shewing secret wit.

XL
He, at his first incomming, charg'd his spere
At him that first appeared in his sight:
That was to weet the stout Sir Sangliere,
Who well was knowen to be a valiant knight,
Approved oft in many a perlous fight.
Him at the first encounter downe he smote,
And overbore beyond his crouper quight,
And after him another knight, that hote
Sir Brianor, so sore, that none him life behote.

XLI
Then, ere his hand he reard, he overthrew
Seven knights, one after other, as they came:
And when his speare was brust, his sword he drew,
The instrument of wrath, and with the same
Far'd like a lyon in his bloodie game,
Hewing and slashing shields and helmets bright,
And beating downe what ever nigh him came,
That every one gan shun his dreadfull sight,
No lesse then death it selfe, in daungerous affright.

XLII
Much wondred all men, what, or whence he came,
That did amongst the troupes so tyrannize;
And each of other gan inquire his name.
But when they could not learne it by no wize,
Most answerable to his wyld disguize
It seemed, him to terme the Salvage Knight.
But certes his right name was otherwize,
Though knowne to few that Arthegall he hight,
The doughtiest knight that liv'd that day, and most of might.

XLIII
Thus was Sir Satyrane with all his band
By his sole manhood and atchievement stout
Dismayd, that none of them in field durst stand,
But beaten were, and chased all about
So he continued all that day throughout,
Till evening, that the sunne gan downward bend.
Then rushed forth out of the thickest rout
A stranger knight, that did his glorie shend:
So nought may be esteemed happie till the end.

XLIV
He at his entrance charg'd his powerfull speare
At Artegall, in middest of his pryde,
And therewith smote him on his umbriere
So sore, that, tombling backe, he downe did slyde
Over his horses taile above a stryde:

Whence litle lust he had to rise againe.
Which Cambell seeing, much the same envyde,
And ran at him with all his might and maine;
But shortly was likewise seene lying on the plaine.

XLV
Whereat full inly wroth was Triamond,
And cast t' avenge the shame doen to his freend:
But by his friend himselfe eke soone he fond,
In no lesse neede of helpe then him he weend.
All which when Blandamour from end to end
Beheld, he woxe therewith displeased sore,
And thought in mind it shortly to amend:
His speare he feutred, and at him it bore;
But with no better fortune then the rest afore.

XLVI
Full many others at him likewise ran:
But all of them likewise dismounted were.
Ne certes wonder; for no powre of man
Could bide the force of that enchaunted speare,
The which this famous Britomart did beare;
With which she wondrous deeds of arms atchieved,
And overthrew what ever came her neare,
That all those stranger knights full sore agrieved,
And that late weaker band of chalengers relieved.

XLVII
Like as in sommers day, when raging heat
Doth burne the earth, and boyled rivers drie,
That all brute beasts, forst to refraine fro meat,
Doe hunt for shade, where shrowded they may lie,
And missing it, faine from themselves to flie;
All travellers tormented are with paine:
A watry cloud doth overcast the skie,
And poureth forth a sudden shoure of raine,
That all the wretched world recomforteth againe.

XLVIII
So did the warlike Britomart restore
The prize to Knights of Maydenhead that day,
Which else was like to have bene lost, and bore
The prayse of prowesse from them all away.
Then shrilling trompets loudly gan to bray,
And bad them leave their labours and long toyle
To joyous feast and other gentle play,
Where beauties prize shold win that pretious spoyle:
Where I with sound of trompe will also rest a whyle.

CANTO V

The ladies for the girdle strive
Of famous Florimell:
Scudamour, comming to Cares house,
Doth sleepe from him expell.

I
It hath bene through all ages ever seene,
That with the praise of armes and chevalrie
The prize of beautie still hath joyned beene;
And that for reasons speciall privitie:
For either doth on other much relie.
For he me seemes most fit the faire to serve,
That can her best defend from villenie;
And she most fit his service doth deserve,
That fairest is and from her faith will never swerve.

II
So fitly now here commeth next in place,
After the proofe of prowesse ended well,
The controverse of beauties soveraine grace;
In which, to her that doth the most excell
Shall fall the girdle of faire Florimell:
That many wish to win for glorie vaine,
And not for vertuous use, which some doe tell
That glorious belt did in it selfe containe,
Which ladies ought to love, and seeke for to obtaine.

III
That girdle gave the vertue of chast love
And wivehood true to all that did it beare;
But whosoever contrarie doth prove
Might not the same about her middle weare:
But it would loose, or else a sunder teare.
Whilome it was (as Faeries wont report)
Dame Venus girdle, by her steemed deare,
What time she usd to live in wively sort;
But layd aside, when so she usd her looser sport.

IV
Her husband Vulcan whylome for her sake,
When first he loved her with heart entire,
This pretious ornament, they say, did make,
And wrought in Lemno with unquenched fire:
And afterwards did for her loves first hire
Give it to her, for ever to remaine,
Therewith to bind lascivious desire,
And loose affections streightly to restraine;

Which vertue it for ever after did retaine.

V

The same one day, when she her selfe disposd
To visite her beloved paramoure,
The God of Warre, she from her middle loosd,
And left behind her in her secret bowre,
On Acidalian mount, where many an howre
She with the pleasant Graces wont to play.
There Florimell in her first ages flowre
Was fostered by those Graces, (as they say)
And brought with her from thence that goodly belt away.

VI

That goodly belt was Cestus hight by name,
And as her life by her esteemed deare.
No wonder then, if that to winne the same
So many ladies sought, as shall appeare;
For pearelesse she was thought, that did it beare.
And now by this their feast all being ended,
The judges which thereto selected were
Into the Martian field adowne descended,
To deeme this doutfull case, for which they all contended.

VII

But first was question made, which of those knights
That lately turneyd had the wager wonne:
There was it judged by those worthie wights,
That Satyrane the first day best had donne:
For he last ended, having first begonne.
The second was to Triamond behight,
For that he sav'd the victour from fordonne:
For Cambell victour was in all mens sight,
Till by mishap he in foemens hand did light.

VIII

The third dayes prize unto that straunger knight,
Whom all men term'd Knight of the Hebene Speare,
To Britomart, was given by good right;
For that with puissant stroke she downe did beare
The Salvage Knight, that victour was whileare,
And all the rest which had the best afore,
And to the last unconquer'd did appeare;
For last is deemed best. To her therefore
The fayrest ladie was adjudgd for paramore.

IX

But thereat greatly grudged Arthegall,
And much repynd, that both of victors meede
And eke of honour she did him forestall.
Yet mote he not withstand what was decreede;

But inly thought of that despightfull deede
Fit time t' awaite avenged for to bee.
This being ended thus, and all agreed,
Then next ensew'd the paragon to see
Of beauties praise, and yeeld the fayrest her due fee.

X
Then first Cambello brought unto their view
His faire Cambina, covered with a veale;
Which being once withdrawne, most perfect hew
And passing beautie did eftsoones reveale,
That able was weake harts away to steale.
Next did Sir Triamond unto their sight
The face of his deare Canacee unheale;
Whose beauties beame eftsoones did shine so bright,
That daz'd the eyes of all, as with exceeding light.

XI
And after her did Paridell produce
His false Duessa, that she might be seene,
Who with her forged beautie did seduce
The hearts of some, that fairest her did weene;
As diverse wits affected divers beene.
Then did Sir Ferramont unto them shew
His Lucida, that was full faire and sheene:
And after these an hundred ladies moe
Appear'd in place, the which each other did outgoe.

XII
All which who so dare thinke for to enchace,
Him needeth sure a golden pen, I weene,
To tell the feature of each goodly face.
For since the day that they created beene,
So many heavenly faces were not seene
Assembled in one place: ne he that thought
For Chian folke to pourtraict beauties queene,
By view of all the fairest to him brought,
So many faire did see, as here he might have sought.

XIII
At last, the most redoubted Britonesse
Her lovely Amoret did open shew;
Whose face discovered, plainely did expresse
The heavenly pourtraict of bright angels hew.
Well weened all, which her that time did vew,
That she should surely beare the bell away,
Till Blandamour, who thought he had the trew
And very Florimell, did her display:
The sight of whom once seene did all the rest dismay.

XIV

For all afore that seemed fayre and bright,
Now base and contemptible did appeare,
Compar'd to her, that shone as Phebes light
Amongst the lesser starres in evening cleare.
All that her saw with wonder ravisht weare,
And weend no mortall creature she should bee,
But some celestiall shape, that flesh did beare:
Yet all were glad there Florimell to see;
Yet thought that Florimell was not so faire as shee.

XV
As guilefull goldsmith that, by secret skill,
With golden foyle doth finely over spred
Some baser metall, which commend he will
Unto the vulgar for good gold insted,
He much more goodly glosse thereon doth shed,
To hide his falshood, then if it were trew:
So hard this idole was to be ared,
That Florimell her selfe in all mens vew
She seem'd to passe: so forged things do fairest shew.

XVI
Then was that golden belt by doome of all
Graunted to her, as to the fayrest dame.
Which being brought, about her middle small
They thought to gird, as best it her became;
But by no meanes they could it thereto frame.
For, ever as they fastned it, it loos'd
And fell away, as feeling secret blame.
Full oft about her wast she it enclos'd;
And it as oft was from about her wast disclos'd.

XVII
That all men wondred at the uncouth sight,
And each one thought as to their fancies came.
But she her selfe did thinke it doen for spight,
And touched was with secret wrath and shame
Therewith, as thing deviz'd her to defame.
Then many other ladies likewise tride
About their tender loynes to knit the same;
But it would not on none of them abide,
But when they thought it fast, eftsoones it was untide.

XVIII
Which when that scornefull Squire of Dames did vew,
He lowdly gan to laugh, and thus to jest:
'Alas for pittie, that so faire a crew,
As like can not be seene from east to west,
Cannot find one this girdle to invest!
Fie on the man that did it first invent,
To shame us all with this, Ungirt unblest!

Let never ladie to his love assent,
That hath this day so many so unmanly shent.'

XIX

Thereat all knights gan laugh, and ladies lowre:
Till that at last the gentle Amoret
Likewise assayd, to prove that girdles powre;
And having it about her middle set,
Did find it fit withouten breach or let.
Whereat the rest gan greatly to envie:
But Florimell exceedingly did fret,
And snatching from her hand halfe angrily
The belt againe, about her bodie gan it tie.

XX

Yet nathemore would it her bodie fit;
Yet nathelesse to her, as her dew right,
It yeelded was by them that judged it:
And she her selfe adjudged to the knight
That bore the hebene speare, as wonne in fight.
But Britomart would not thereto assent,
Ne her owne Amoret forgoe so light
For that strange dame, whose beauties wonderment
She lesse esteem'd then th' others vertuous government.

XXI

Whom when the rest did see her to refuse,
They were full glad, in hope themselves to get her:
Yet at her choice they all did greatly muse.
But after that, the judges did arret her
Unto the second best, that lov'd her better;
That was the Salvage Knight: but he was gone
In great displeasure, that he could not get her.
Then was she judged Triamond his one;
But Triamond lov'd Canacee, and other none.

XXII

Tho unto Satyran she was adjudged,
Who was right glad to gaine so goodly meed:
But Blandamour thereat full greatly grudged,
And litle prays'd his labours evill speed,
That, for to winne the saddle, lost the steed.
Ne lesse thereat did Paridell complaine,
And thought t' appeale from that which was decreed
To single combat with Sir Satyrane.
Thereto him Ate stird, new discord to maintaine.

XXIII

And eke with these, full many other knights
She through her wicked working did incense,
Her to demaund, and chalenge as their rights,

Deserved for their perils recompense.
Amongst the rest, with boastfull vaine pretense
Stept Braggadochio forth, and as his thrall
Her claym'd, by him in battell wonne long sens:
Whereto her selfe he did to witnesse call;
Who being askt, accordingly confessed all.

XXIV
Thereat exceeding wroth was Satyran;
And wroth with Satyran was Blandamour;
And wroth with Blandamour was Erivan;
And at them both Sir Paridell did loure.
So all together stird up strifull stoure,
And readie were new battell to darraine.
Each one profest to be her paramoure,
And vow'd with speare and shield it to maintaine;
Ne judges powre, ne reasons rule, mote them restraine.

XXV
Which troublous stirre when Satyrane aviz'd,
He gan to cast how to appease the same,
And, to accord them all, this meanes deviz'd:
First in the midst to set that fayrest dame,
To whom each one his chalenge should disclame,
And he himselfe his right would eke releasse:
Then looke, to whom she voluntarie came,
He should without disturbance her possesse:
Sweete is the love that comes alone with willingnesse.

XXVI
They all agreed, and then that snowy mayd
Was in the middest plast among them all:
All on her gazing wisht, and vowd, and prayd,
And to the Queene of Beautie close did call,
That she unto their portion might befall.
Then when she long had lookt upon each one,
As though she wished to have pleasd them all,
At last to Braggadochio selfe alone
She came of her accord, in spight of all his fone.

XXVII
Which when they all beheld, they chaft, and rag'd,
And woxe nigh mad for very harts despight,
That from revenge their willes they scarse asswag'd:
Some thought from him her to have reft by might;
Some proffer made with him for her to fight.
But he nought car'd for all that they could say:
For he their words as wind esteemed light.
Yet not fit place he thought it there to stay,
But secretly from thence that night her bore away.

XXVIII
They which remaynd, so soone as they perceiv'd
That she was gone, departed thence with speed,
And follow'd them, in mind her to have reav'd
From wight unworthie of so noble meed.
In which poursuit how each one did succeede,
Shall else be told in order, as it fell.
But now of Britomart it here doth neede,
The hard adventures and strange haps to tell;
Since with the rest she went not after Florimell.

XXIX
For soone as she them saw to discord set,
Her list no longer in that place abide;
But taking with her lovely Amoret,
Upon her first adventure forth did ride,
To seeke her lov'd, making blind Love her guide.
Unluckie mayd, to seeke her enemie!
Unluckie mayd, to seeke him farre and wide,
Whom, when he was unto her selfe most nie,
She through his late disguizement could him not descrie!

XXX
So much the more her griefe, the more her toyle:
Yet neither toyle nor griefe she once did spare,
In seeking him that should her paine assoyle;
Whereto great comfort in her sad misfare
Was Amoret, companion of her care:
Who likewise sought her lover long miswent,
The gentle Scudamour, whose hart whileare
That stryfull hag with gealous discontent
Had fild, that he to fell reveng was fully bent.

XXXI
Bent to revenge on blamelesse Britomart
The crime which cursed Ate kindled earst,
The which like thornes did pricke his gealous hart,
And through his soule like poysned arrow perst,
That by no reason it might be reverst,
For ought that Glauce could or doe or say.
For aye the more that she the same reherst,
The more it gauld and griev'd him night and day,
That nought but dire revenge his anger mote defray.

XXXII
So as they travelled, the drouping night,
Covered with cloudie storme and bitter showre,
That dreadfull seem'd to every living wight,
Upon them fell, before her timely howre;
That forced them to seeke some covert bowre,
Where they might hide their heads in quiet rest,

And shrowd their persons from that stormie stowre.
Not farre away, not meete for any guest,
They spide a little cottage, like some poore mans nest.

XXXIII
Under a steepe hilles side it placed was,
There where the mouldred earth had cav'd the banke;
And fast beside a little brooke did pas
Of muddie water, that like puddle stanke,
By which few crooked sallowes grew in ranke:
Wherto approaching nigh, they heard the sound
Of many yron hammers beating ranke,
And answering their wearie turnes around,
That seemed some blacksmith dwelt in that desert ground.

XXXIV
There entring in, they found the goodman selfe
Full busily unto his worke ybent;
Who was to weet a wretched wearish elfe,
With hollow eyes and rawbone cheekes forspent,
As if he had in prison long bene pent:
Full blacke and griesly did his face appeare,
Besmeard with smoke that nigh his eyesight blent;
With rugged beard, and hoarie shagged heare,
The which he never wont to combe, or comely sheare.

XXXV
Rude was his garment, and to rags all rent,
Ne better had he, ne for better cared:
With blistred hands emongst the cinders brent,
And fingers filthie, with long nayles unpared,
Right fit to rend the food on which he fared.
His name was Care; a blacksmith by his trade,
That neither day nor night from working spared,
But to small purpose yron wedges made;
Those be unquiet thoughts, that carefull minds invade.

XXXVI
In which his worke he had sixe servants prest,
About the andvile standing evermore,
With huge great hammers, that did never rest
From heaping stroakes, which thereon soused sore:
All sixe strong groomes, but one then other more:
For by degrees they all were disagreed;
So likewise did the hammers which they bore
Like belles in greatnesse orderly succeed,
That he which was the last the first did farre exceede.

XXXVII
He like a monstrous gyant seem'd in sight,
Farre passing Bronteus or Pyracmon great,

The which in Lipari doe day and night
Frame thunderbolts for Joves avengefull threate.
So dreadfully he did the andvile beat,
That seem'd to dust he shortly would it drive:
So huge his hammer and so fierce his heat,
That seem'd a rocke of diamond it could rive,
And rend a sunder quite, if he thereto list strive.

XXXVIII
Sir Scudamour, there entring, much admired
The manner of their worke and wearie paine;
And having long beheld, at last enquired
The cause and end thereof: but all in vaine;
For they for nought would from their worke refraine,
Ne let his speeches come unto their eare;
And eke the breathfull bellowes blew amaine,
Like to the northren winde, that none could heare:
Those Pensifenesse did move; and Sighes the bellows weare.

XXXIX
Which when that warriour saw, he said no more,
But in his armour layd him downe to rest:
To rest he layd him downe upon the flore,
(Whylome for ventrous knights the bedding best,)
And thought his wearie limbs to have redrest.
And that old aged dame, his faithfull squire,
Her feeble joynts layd eke a downe to rest;
That needed much her weake age to desire,
After so long a travell, which them both did tire.

XL
There lay Sir Scudamour long while expecting.
When gentle sleepe his heavie eyes would close;
Oft chaunging sides, and oft new place electing,
Where better seem'd he mote himselfe repose;
And oft in wrath he thence againe uprose;
And oft in wrath he layd him downe againe.
But wheresoever he did himselfe dispose,
He by no meanes could wished ease obtaine:
So every place seem'd painefull, and ech changing vaine.

XLI
And evermore, when he to sleepe did thinke,
The hammers sound his senses did molest;
And evermore, when he began to winke,
The bellowes noyse disturb'd his quiet rest,
Ne suffred sleepe to settle in his brest.
And all the night the dogs did barke and howle
About the house, at sent of stranger guest:
And now the crowing cocke, and now the owle
Lowde shriking, him afflicted to the very sowle.

XLII
And if by fortune any litle nap
Upon his heavie eye-lids chaunst to fall,
Eftsoones one of those villeins him did rap
Upon his headpeece with his yron mall,
That he was soone awaked therewithall,
And lightly started up as one affrayd,
Or as if one him suddenly did call:
So oftentimes he out of sleepe abrayd,
And then lay musing long on that him ill apayd.

XLIII
So long he muzed, and so long he lay,
That at the last his wearie sprite opprest
With fleshly weaknesse, which no creature may
Long time resist, gave place to kindly rest,
That all his senses did full soone arrest:
Yet, in his soundest sleepe, his dayly feare
His ydle braine gan busily molest,
And made him dreame those two disloyall were:
The things that day most minds, at night doe most appeare.

XLIV
With that, the wicked carle, the maister smith,
A paire of redwhote yron tongs did take
Out of the burning cinders, and therewith
Under his side him nipt, that, forst to wake,
He felt his hart for very paine to quake,
And started up avenged for to be
On him the which his quiet slomber brake:
Yet, looking round about him, none could see;
Yet did the smart remaine, though he himselfe did flee.

XLV
In such disquiet and hartfretting payne
He all that night, that too long night, did passe.
And now the day out of the ocean mayne
Began to peepe above this earthly masse,
With pearly dew sprinkling the morning grasse:
Then up he rose like heavie lumpe of lead,
That in his face, as in a looking glasse,
The signes of anguish one mote plainely read,
And ghesse the man to be dismayd with gealous dread.

XLVI
Unto his lofty steede he clombe anone,
And forth upon his former voiage fared,
And with him eke that aged squire attone;
Who, whatsoever perill was prepared,
Both equall paines and equall perill shared:

The end whereof and daungerous event
Shall for another canticle be spared:
But here my wearie teeme, nigh over spent,
Shall breath it selfe awhile, after so long a went.

CANTO VI

**Both Scudamour and Arthegall
Doe fight with Britomart:
He sees her face; doth fall in love,
And soone from her depart.**

I
What equall torment to the griefe of mind,
And pyning anguish hid in gentle hart,
That inly feeds it selfe with thoughts unkind,
And nourisheth her owne consuming smart?
What medicine can any leaches art
Yeeld such a sore, that doth her grievance hide,
And will to none her maladie impart?
Such was the wound that Scudamour did gride;
For which Dan Phebus selfe cannot a salve provide.

II
Who having left that restlesse House of Care,
The next day, as he on his way did ride,
Full of melancholie and sad misfare,
Through misconceipt, all unawares espide
An armed knight under a forrest side,
Sitting in shade beside his grazing steede;
Who, soone as them approaching he descride,
Gan towards them to pricke with eger speede,
That seem'd he was full bent to some mischievous deede.

III
Which Scudamour perceiving, forth issewed
To have rencountred him in equall race;
But soone as th' other, nigh approaching, vewed
The armes he bore, his speare he gan abase,
And voide his course: at which so suddain case
He wondred much. But th' other thus can say:
'Ah! gentle Scudamour, unto your grace
I me submit, and you of pardon pray,
That almost had against you trespassed this day.'

IV
Whereto thus Scudamour: 'Small harme it were

For any knight upon a ventrous knight
Without displeasance for to prove his spere.
But reade you, sir, sith ye my name have hight,
What is your owne, that I mote you requite?'
'Certes,' sayd he, 'ye mote as now excuse
Me from discovering you my name aright:
For time yet serves that I the same refuse;
But call ye me the Salvage Knight, as others use.'

V
'Then this, Sir Salvage Knight,' quoth he, 'areede;
Or doe you here within this forrest wonne,
That seemeth well to answere to your weede?
Or have ye it for some occasion donne?
That rather seemes, sith knowen armes ye shonne.'
'This other day,' sayd he, 'a stranger knight
Shame and dishonour hath unto me donne;
On whom I waite to wreake that foule despight,
When ever he this way shall passe by day or night.'

VI
'Shame be his meede,' quoth he, 'that meaneth shame.
But what is he by whom ye shamed were?'
'A stranger knight,' sayd he, 'unknowne by name,
But knowne by fame, and by an hebene speare,
With which he all that met him downe did beare.
He in an open turney, lately held,
Fro me the honour of that game did reare;
And having me, all wearie earst, downe feld,
The fayrest ladie reft, and ever since withheld.'

VII
When Scudamour heard mention of that speare,
He wist right well that it was Britomart,
The which from him his fairest love did beare.
Tho gan he swell in every inner part,
For fell despight, and gnaw his gealous hart,
That thus he sharply sayd: 'Now by my head,
Yet is not this the first unknightly part,
Which that same knight, whom by his launce I read,
Hath doen to noble knights, that many makes him dread.

VIII
'For lately he my love hath fro me reft,
And eke defiled with foule villanie
The sacred pledge which in his faith was left,
In shame of knighthood and fidelitie;
The which ere long full deare he shall abie.
And if to that avenge by you decreed
This hand may helpe, or succour aught supplie,
It shall not fayle, when so ye shall it need.'

So both to wreake their wrathes on Britomart agreed.

IX
Whiles thus they communed, lo! farre away
A knight soft ryding towards them they spyde,
Attyr'd in forraine armes and straunge aray:
Whom when they nigh approcht, they plaine descryde
To be the same for whom they did abyde.
Sayd then Sir Scudamour, 'Sir Salvage Knight,
Let me this crave, sith first I was defyde,
That first I may that wrong to him requite:
And, if I hap to fayle, you shall recure my right.'

X
Which being yeelded, he his threatfull speare
Gan fewter, and against her fiercely ran.
Who soone as she him saw approaching neare
With so fell rage, her selfe she lightly gan
To dight, to welcome him well as she can:
But entertaind him in so rude a wise,
That to the ground she smote both horse and man;
Whence neither greatly hasted to arise,
But on their common harmes together did devise.

XI
But Artegall, beholding his mischaunce,
New matter added to his former fire;
And eft aventring his steeleheaded launce,
Against her rode, full of despiteous ire,
That nought but spoyle and vengeance did require.
But to himselfe his felonous intent
Returning, disappointed his desire,
Whiles unawares his saddle he forwent,
And found himselfe on ground in great amazement.

XII
Lightly he started up out of that stound,
And snatching forth his direfull deadly blade,
Did leape to her, as doth an eger hound
Thrust to an hynd within some covert glade,
Whom without perill he cannot invade.
With such fell greedines he her assayled,
That though she mounted were, yet he her made
To give him ground, (so much his force prevayled)
And shun his mightie strokes, gainst which no armes avayled.

XIII
So as they coursed here and there, it chaunst
That, in her wheeling round, behind her crest
So sorely he her strooke, that thence it glaunst
Adowne her backe, the which it fairely blest

From foule mischance; ne did it ever rest,
Till on her horses hinder parts it fell;
Where byting deepe, so deadly it imprest,
That quite it chynd his backe behind the sell,
And to alight on foote her algates did compell.

XIV

Like as the lightning brond from riven skie,
Throwne out by angry Jove in his vengeance,
With dreadfull force falles on some steeple hie;
Which battring, downe it on the church doth glance,
And teares it all with terrible mischance.
Yet she no whit dismayd, her steed forsooke,
And casting from her that enchaunted lance,
Unto her sword and shield her soone betooke;
And therewithall at him right furiously she strooke.

XV

So furiously she strooke in her first heat,
Whiles with long fight on foot he breathlesse was,
That she him forced backward to retreat,
And yeeld unto her weapon way to pas:
Whose raging rigour neither steele nor bras
Could stay, but to the tender flesh it went,
And pour'd the purple bloud forth on the gras;
That all his mayle yriv'd, and plates yrent,
Shew'd all his bodie bare unto the cruell dent.

XVI

At length, when as he saw her hastie heat
Abate, and panting breath begin to fayle,
He, through long sufferance growing now more great,
Rose in his strength, and gan her fresh assayle,
Heaping huge strokes, as thicke as showre of hayle,
And lashing dreadfully at every part,
As if he thought her soule to disentrayle.
Ah! cruell hand, and thrise more cruell hart,
That workst such wrecke on her to whom thou dearest art!

XVII

What yron courage ever could endure,
To worke such outrage on so faire a creature?
And in his madnesse thinke with hands impure
To spoyle so goodly workmanship of nature,
The Maker selfe resembling in her feature?
Certes some hellish furie, or some feend,
This mischiefe framd, for their first loves defeature,
To bath their hands in bloud of dearest freend,
Thereby to make their loves beginning their lives end.

XVIII

Thus long they trac'd and traverst to and fro,
Sometimes pursewing, and sometimes pursewed,
Still as advantage they espyde thereto:
But toward th' end Sir Arthegall renewed
His strength still more, but she still more decrewed.
At last his lucklesse hand he heav'd on hie,
Having his forces all in one accrewed,
And therewith stroke at her so hideouslie,
That seemed nought but death mote be her destinie.

XIX
The wicked stroke upon her helmet chaunst,
And with the force which in it selfe it bore
Her ventayle shard away, and thence forth glaunst
Adowne in vaine, ne harm'd her any more.
With that, her angels face, unseene afore,
Like to the ruddie morne appeard in sight,
Deawed with silver drops, through sweating sore,
But somewhat redder then beseem'd aright,
Through toylesome heate and labour of her weary fight.

XX
And round about the same, her yellow heare,
Having through stirring loosd their wonted band,
Like to a golden border did appeare,
Framed in goldsmithes forge with cunning hand:
Yet goldsmithes cunning could not understand
To frame such subtile wire, so shinie cleare.
For it did glister like the golden sand,
The which Pactolus, with his waters shere,
Throwes forth upon the rivage round about him nere.

XXI
And as his hand he up againe did reare,
Thinking to worke on her his utmost wracke,
His powrelesse arme, benumbd with secret feare,
From his revengefull purpose shronke abacke,
And cruell sword out of his fingers slacke
Fell downe to ground, as if the steele had sence,
And felt some ruth, or sence his hand did lacke,
Or both of them did thinke, obedience
To doe to so divine a beauties excellence.

XXII
And he himselfe long gazing thereupon,
At last fell humbly downe upon his knee,
And of his wonder made religion,
Weening some heavenly goddesse he did see,
Or else unweeting what it else might bee;
And pardon her besought his errour frayle,
That had done outrage in so high degree:

Whilest trembling horrour did his sense assayle,
And made ech member quake, and manly hart to quayle.

XXIII
Nathelesse she, full of wrath for that late stroke,
All that long while upheld her wrathfull hand,
With fell intent on him to bene ywroke:
And looking sterne, still over him did stand,
Threatning to strike, unlesse he would withstand:
And bad him rise, or surely he should die.
But, die or live, for nought he would upstand,
But her of pardon prayd more earnestlie,
Or wreake on him her will for so great injurie.

XXIV
Which when as Scudamour, who now abrayd,
Beheld, where as he stood not farre aside,
He was therewith right wondrously dismayd,
And drawing nigh, when as he plaine descride
That peerelesse paterne of Dame Natures pride,
And heavenly image of perfection,
He blest himselfe, as one sore terrifide,
And turning feare to faint devotion,
Did worship her as some celestiall vision.

XXV
But Glauce, seeing all that chaunced there,
Well weeting how their errour to assoyle,
Full glad of so good end, to them drew nere,
And her salewd with seemly belaccoyle,
Joyous to see her safe after long toyle:
Then her besought, as she to her was deare,
To graunt unto those warriours truce a whyle;
Which yeelded, they their bevers up did reare,
And shew'd themselves to her, such as indeed they were.

XXVI
When Britomart with sharpe avizefull eye
Beheld the lovely face of Artegall,
Tempred with sternesse and stout majestie,
She gan eftsoones it to her mind to call,
To be the same which in her fathers hall
Long since in that enchaunted glasse she saw.
Therewith her wrathfull courage gan appall,
And haughtie spirits meekely to adaw,
That her enhaunced hand she downe can soft withdraw.

XXVII
Yet she it forst to have againe upheld,
As fayning choler, which was turn'd to cold:
But ever when his visage she beheld,

Her hand fell downe, and would no longer hold
The wrathfull weapon gainst his countnance bold:
But when in vaine to fight she oft assayd,
She arm'd her tongue, and thought at him to scold;
Nathlesse her tongue not to her will obayd,
But brought forth speeches myld, when she would have missayd.

XXVIII
But Scudamour now woxen inly glad,
That all his gealous feare he false had found,
And how that hag his love abused had
With breach of faith and loyaltie unsound,
The which long time his grieved hart did wound,
Him thus bespake: 'Certes, Sir Artegall,
I joy to see you lout so low on ground,
And now become to live a ladies thrall,
That whylome in your minde wont to despise them all.'

XXIX
Soone as she heard the name of Artegall,
Her hart did leape, and all her hart-strings tremble,
For sudden joy, and secret feare withall,
And all her vitall powres, with motion nimble,
To succour it, themselves gan there assemble,
That by the swift recourse of flushing blood
Right plaine appeard, though she it would dissemble,
And fayned still her former angry mood,
Thinking to hide the depth by troubling of the flood.

XXX
When Glauce thus gan wisely all upknit:
'Ye gentle knights, whom fortune here hath brought,
To be spectators of this uncouth fit,
Which secret fate hath in this ladie wrought,
Against the course of kind, ne mervaile nought,
Ne thenceforth feare the thing that hether-too
Hath troubled both your mindes with idle thought,
Fearing least she your loves away should woo,
Feared in vaine, sith meanes ye see there wants theretoo.

XXXI
'And you, Sir Artegall, the Salvage Knight,
Henceforth may not disdaine that womans hand
Hath conquered you anew in second fight:
For whylome they have conquerd sea and land,
And heaven it selfe, that nought may them withstand:
Ne henceforth be rebellious unto love,
That is the crowne of knighthood, and the band
Of noble minds derived from above,
Which being knit with vertue, never will remove.

XXXII

'And you, faire ladie knight, my dearest dame,
Relent the rigour of your wrathfull will,
Whose fire were better turn'd to other flame;
And wiping out remembrance of all ill,
Graunt him your grace, but so that he fulfill
The penance which ye shall to him empart:
For lovers heaven must passe by sorrowes hell.'
Thereat full inly blushed Britomart;
But Artegall, close smyling, joy'd in secret hart.

XXXIII

Yet durst he not make love so suddenly,
Ne thinke th' affection of her hart to draw
From one to other so quite contrary:
Besides her modest countenance he saw
So goodly grave, and full of princely aw,
That it his ranging fancie did refraine,
And looser thoughts to lawfull bounds withdraw;
Whereby the passion grew more fierce and faine,
Like to a stubborne steede whom strong hand would restraine.

XXXIV

But Scudamour, whose hart twixt doubtfull feare
And feeble hope hung all this while suspence,
Desiring of his Amoret to heare
Some gladfull newes and sure intelligence,
Her thus bespake: 'But, sir, without offence
Mote I request you tydings of my love,
My Amoret, sith you her freed fro thence,
Where she, captived long, great woes did prove;
That where ye left, I may her seeke, as doth behove.'

XXXV

To whom thus Britomart: 'Certes, sir knight,
What is of her become, or whether reft,
I can not unto you aread a right.
For from that time I from enchaunters theft
Her freed, in which ye her all hopelesse left,
I her preserv'd from perill and from feare,
And evermore from villenie her kept:
Ne ever was there wight to me more deare
Then she, ne unto whom I more true love did beare.

XXXVI

'Till on a day, as through a desert wyld
We travelled, both wearie of the way,
We did alight, and sate in shadow myld;
Where fearelesse I to sleepe me downe did lay.
But when as I did out of sleepe abray,
I found her not where I her left whyleare,

But thought she wandred was, or gone astray.
I cal'd her loud, I sought her farre and neare;
But no where could her find, nor tydings of her heare.'

XXXVII
When Scudamour those heavie tydings heard,
His hart was thrild with point of deadly feare;
Ne in his face or bloud or life appeard,
But senselesse stood, like to a mazed steare
That yet of mortall stroke the stound doth beare;
Till Glauce thus: 'Faire sir, be nought dismayd
With needelesse dread, till certaintie ye heare:
For yet she may be safe though somewhat strayd;
Its best to hope the best, though of the worst affrayd.'

XXXVIII
Nathlesse he hardly of her chearefull speech
Did comfort take, or in his troubled sight
Shew'd change of better cheare, so sore a breach
That sudden newes had made into his spright;
Till Britomart him fairely thus behight:
'Great cause of sorrow certes, sir, ye have:
But comfort take: for by this heavens light
I vow, you dead or living not to leave,
Till I her find, and wreake on him that did her reave.'

XXXIX
Therewith he rested, and well pleased was.
So peace being confirm'd amongst them all,
They tooke their steeds, and forward thence did pas
Unto some resting place, which mote befall,
All being guided by Sir Artegall:
Where goodly solace was unto them made,
And dayly feasting both in bowre and hall,
Untill that they their wounds well healed had,
And wearie limmes recur'd after late usage bad.

XL
In all which time, Sir Artegall made way
Unto the love of noble Britomart,
And with meeke service and much suit did lay
Continuall siege unto her gentle hart:
Which being whylome launcht with lovely dart,
More eath was new impression to receive,
How ever she her paynd with womanish art
To hide her wound, that none might it perceive:
Vaine is the art that seekes it selfe for to deceive.

XLI
So well he woo'd her, and so well he wrought her,
With faire entreatie and sweet blandishment,

That at the length unto a bay he brought her,
So as she to his speeches was content
To lend an eare, and softly to relent.
At last, through many vowes which forth he pour'd,
And many othes, she yeelded her consent
To be his love, and take him for her lord,
Till they with mariage meet might finish that accord.

XLII
Tho, when they had long time there taken rest,
Sir Artegall, who all this while was bound
Upon an hard adventure yet in quest,
Fit time for him thence to depart it found,
To follow that which he did long propound;
And unto her his congee came to take.
But her therewith full sore displeasd he found,
And loth to leave her late betrothed make,
Her dearest love full loth so shortly to forsake.

XLIII
Yet he with strong perswasions her asswaged,
And wonne her will to suffer him depart;
For which his faith with her he fast engaged,
And thousand vowes from bottome of his hart,
That all so soone as he by wit or art
Could that atchieve, whereto he did aspire,
He unto her would speedily revert:
No longer space thereto he did desire,
But till the horned moone three courses did expire.

XLIV
With which she for the present was appeased,
And yeelded leave, how ever malcontent
She inly were, and in her mind displeased.
So, early in the morrow next, he went
Forth on his way, to which he was ybent;
Ne wight him to attend, or way to guide,
As whylome was the custome ancient
Mongst knights, when on adventures they did ride,
Save that she algates him a while accompanide.

XLV
And by the way she sundry purpose found
Of this or that, the time for to delay,
And of the perils whereto he was bound,
The feare whereof seem'd much her to affray:
But all she did was but to weare out day.
Full oftentimes she leave of him did take;
And eft againe deviz'd some what to say,
Which she forgot, whereby excuse to make:
So loth she was his companie for to forsake.

XLVI

At last, when all her speeches she had spent,
And new occasion fayld her more to find,
She left him to his fortunes government,
And backe returned with right heavie mind
To Scudamour, who she had left behind:
With whom she went to seeke faire Amoret,
Her second care, though in another kind:
For vertues onely sake, which doth beget
True love and faithfull friendship, she by her did set.

XLVII

Backe to that desert forrest they retyred,
Where sorie Britomart had lost her late;
There they her sought, and every where inquired,
Where they might tydings get of her estate;
Yet found they none. But by what haplesse fate
Or hard misfortune she was thence convayd,
And stolne away from her beloved mate,
Were long to tell; therefore I here will stay
Untill another tyde, that I it finish may.

CANTO VII

Amoret rapt by greedie Lust
Belphebe saves from dread:
The squire her loves, and being blam'd,
His dayes in dole doth lead.

I

Great God of Love, that with thy cruell darts
Doest conquer greatest conquerors on ground,
And setst thy kingdome in the captive harts
Of kings and keasars, to thy service bound,
What glorie or what guerdon hast thou found
In feeble ladies tyranning so sore,
And adding anguish to the bitter wound,
With which their lives thou lanchedst long afore,
By heaping stormes of trouble on them daily more?

II

So whylome didst thou to faire Florimell;
And so and so to noble Britomart:
So doest thou now to her of whom I tell,
The lovely Amoret, whose gentle hart
Thou martyrest with sorow and with smart,

In salvage forrests and in deserts wide,
With beares and tygers taking heavie part,
Withouten comfort, and withouten guide,
That pittie is to heare the perils which she tride.

III
So soone as she with that brave Britonesse
Had left that turneyment for beauties prise,
They travel'd long; that now for wearinesse,
Both of the way and warlike exercise,
Both through a forest ryding did devise
T' alight, and rest their wearie limbs awhile.
There heavie sleepe the eye-lids did surprise
Of Britomart, after long tedious toyle,
That did her passed paines in quiet rest assoyle.

IV
The whiles faire Amoret, of nought affeard,
Walkt through the wood, for pleasure or for need;
When suddenly behind her backe she heard
One rushing forth out of the thickest weed,
That ere she backe could turne to taken heed,
Had unawares her snatched up from ground.
Feebly she shriekt, but so feebly indeed,
That Britomart heard not the shrilling sound,
There where through weary travel she lay sleeping sound.

V
It was to weet a wilde and salvage man,
Yet was no man, but onely like in shape,
And eke in stature higher by a span,
All overgrowne with haire, that could awhape
An hardy hart, and his wide mouth did gape
With huge great teeth, like to a tusked bore:
For he liv'd all on ravin and on rape
Of men and beasts; and fed on fleshly gore,
The signe whereof yet stain'd his bloudy lips afore.

VI
His neather lip was not like man nor beast,
But like a wide deepe poke, downe hanging low,
In which he wont the relickes of his feast
And cruell spoyle, which he had spard, to stow:
And over it his huge great nose did grow,
Full dreadfully empurpled all with bloud;
And downe both sides two wide long eares did glow,
And raught downe to his waste, when up he stood,
More great then th' eares of elephants by Indus flood.

VII
His wast was with a wreath of yvie greene

Engirt about, ne other garment wore:
For all his haire was like a garment seene;
And in his hand a tall young oake he bore,
Whose knottie snags were sharpned all afore,
And beath'd in fire for steele to be in sted.
But whence he was, or of what wombe ybore,
Of beasts, or of the earth, I have not red:
But certes was with milke of wolves and tygres fed.

VIII
This ugly creature in his armes her snatcht,
And through the forrest bore her quite away,
With briers and bushes all to-rent and scratcht;
Ne care he had, ne pittie of the pray,
Which many a knight had sought so many a day.
He stayed not, but in his armes her bearing
Ran, till he came to th' end of all his way,
Unto his cave, farre from all peoples hearing,
And there he threw her in, nought feeling, ne nought fearing.

IX
For she, deare ladie, all the way was dead,
Whilest he in armes her bore; but when she felt
Her selfe downe soust, she waked out of dread
Streight into griefe, that her deare hart nigh swelt,
And eft gan into tender teares to melt.
Then when she lookt about, and nothing found
But darknesse and dread horrour, where she dwelt,
She almost fell againe into a swound,
Ne wist whether above she were, or under ground.

X
With that she heard some one close by her side
Sighing and sobbing sore, as if the paine
Her tender hart in peeces would divide:
Which she long listning, softly askt againe
What mister wight it was that so did plaine?
To whom thus aunswer'd was: 'Ah, wretched wight!
That seekes to know anothers griefe in vaine,
Unweeting of thine owne like haplesse plight:
Selfe to forget to mind another, is oversight.'

XI
'Aye me!' said she, 'where am I, or with whom?
Emong the living, or emong the dead?
What shall of me, unhappy maid, become?
Shall death be th' end, or ought else worse, aread.'
'Unhappy mayd,' then answer'd she, 'whose dread
Untride is lesse then when thou shalt it try:
Death is to him that wretched life doth lead,
Both grace and gaine; but he in hell doth lie,

That lives a loathed life, and wishing cannot die.

XII
'This dismall day hath thee a caytive made,
And vassall to the vilest wretch alive,
Whose cursed usage and ungodly trade
The heavens abhorre, and into darkenesse drive.
For on the spoile of women he doth live,
Whose bodies chast, when ever in his powre
He may them catch, unable to gainestrive,
He with his shamefull lust doth first deflowre,
And afterwards themselves doth cruelly devoure.

XIII
'Now twenty daies, by which the sonnes of men
Divide their works, have past through heven sheene,
Since I was brought into this dolefull den;
During which space these sory eies have seen
Seaven women by him slaine, and eaten clene.
And now no more for him but I alone,
And this old woman, here remaining beene;
Till thou cam'st hither to augment our mone;
And of us three to morrow he will sure eate one.'

XIV
'Ah! dreadfull tidings which thou doest declare,'
Quoth she, 'of all that ever hath bene knowen!
Full many great calamities and rare
This feeble brest endured hath, but none
Equally to this, where ever I have gone.
But what are you, whom like unlucky lot
Hath linckt with me in the same chaine attone?'
'To tell,' quoth she, 'that which ye see, needs not;
A wofull wretched maid, of God and man forgot.

XV
'But what I was it irkes me to reherse;
Daughter unto a lord of high degree,
That joyd in happy peace, till Fates perverse
With guilefull Love did secretly agree,
To overthrow my state and dignitie.
It was my lot to love a gentle swaine,
Yet was he but a squire of low degree;
Yet was he meet, unlesse mine eye did faine,
By any ladies side for leman to have laine.

XVI
'But, for his meannesse and disparagement,
My sire, who me too dearely well did love,
Unto my choise by no meanes would assent,
But often did my folly fowle reprove.

Yet nothing could my fixed mind remove,
But whether willed or nilled friend or foe,
I me resolv'd the utmost end to prove,
And rather then my love abandon so,
Both sire, and friends, and all for ever to forgo.

XVII
'Thenceforth I sought by secret meanes to worke
Time to my will, and from his wrathfull sight
To hide th' intent which in my heart did lurke,
Till I thereto had all things ready dight.
So on a day, unweeting unto wight,
I with that squire agreede away to flit,
And in a privy place, betwixt us hight,
Within a grove appointed him to meete;
To which I boldly came upon my feeble feete.

XVIII
'But ah! unhappy houre me thither brought:
For in that place where I him thought to find,
There was I found, contrary to my thought,
Of this accursed earle of hellish kind,
The shame of men, and plague of woman-kind;
Who trussing me, as eagle doth his pray,
Me hether brought with him, as swift as wind,
Where yet untouched till this present day,
I rest his wretched thrall, the sad Æmylia.'

XIX
'Ah! sad Æmylia,' then sayd Amoret,
'Thy ruefull plight I pitty as mine owne.
But read to me, by what devise or wit
Hast thou, in all this time, from him unknowne
Thine honor sav'd, though into thraldome throwne?'
'Through helpe,' quoth she, 'of this old woman here
I have so done, as she to me hath showne:
For ever, when he burnt in lustfull fire,
She in my stead supplide his bestiall desire.'

XX
Thus of their evils as they did discourse,
And each did other much bewaile and mone,
Loe! where the villaine selfe, their sorrowes sourse,
Came to the cave, and rolling thence the stone,
Which wont to stop the mouth thereof, that none
Might issue forth, came rudely rushing in,
And spredding over all the flore alone,
Gan dight him selfe unto his wonted sinne;
Which ended, then his bloudy banket should beginne.

XXI

Which when as fearefull Amoret perceoved,
She staid not the utmost end thereof to try,
But like a ghastly gelt, whose wits are reaved,
Ran forth in hast with hideous outcry,
For horrour of his shamefull villany.
But after her full lightly he uprose,
And her pursu'd as fast as she did flie:
Full fast she flies, and farre afore him goes,
Ne feeles the thorns and thickets pricke her tender toes.

XXII
Nor hedge, nor ditch, nor hill, nor dale she staies,
But overleapes them all, like robucke light,
And through the thickest makes her nighest waies;
And evermore when with regardfull sight
She, looking backe, espies that griesly wight
Approching nigh, she gins to mend her pace,
And makes her feare a spur to hast her flight:
More swift then Myrrh' or Daphne in her race,
Or any of the Thracian Nimphes in salvage chase.

XXIII
Long so she fled, and so he follow'd long;
Ne living aide for her on earth appeares,
But if the heavens helpe to redresse her wrong,
Moved with pity of her plenteous teares.
It fortuned, Belphebe with her peares,
The woody nimphs, and with that lovely boy,
Was hunting then the libbards and the beares,
In these wild woods, as was her wonted joy,
To banish sloth, that oft doth noble mindes annoy.

XXIV
It so befell, as oft it fals in chace,
That each of them from other sundred were,
And that same gentle squire arriv'd in place
Where this same cursed caytive did appeare,
Pursuing that faire lady full of feare;
And now he her quite overtaken had;
And now he her away with him did beare
Under his arme, as seeming wondrous glad,
That by his greuning laughter mote farre off be rad.

XXV
Which drery sight the gentle squire espying,
Doth hast to crosse him by the nearest way,
Led with that wofull ladies piteous crying,
And him assailes with all the might he may:
Yet will not he the lovely spoile downe lay,
But with his craggy club in his right hand
Defends him selfe, and saves his gotten pray.

Yet had it bene right hard him to with-stand,
But that he was full light and nimble on the land.

XXVI
Thereto the villaine used craft in fight;
For ever when the squire his javelin shooke,
He held the lady forth before him right,
And with her body, as a buckler, broke
The puissance of his intended stroke.
And if it chaunst, (as needs it must in fight)
Whilest he on him was greedy to be wroke,
That any little blow on her did light,
Then would he laugh aloud, and gather great delight.

XXVII
Which subtill sleight did him encumber much,
And made him oft, when he would strike, forbeare;
For hardly could he come the carle to touch,
But that he her must hurt, or hazard neare:
Yet he his hand so carefully did beare,
That at the last he did himselfe attaine,
And therein left the pike head of his speare.
A streame of coleblacke bloud thence gusht amaine,
That all her silken garments did with bloud bestaine.

XXVIII
With that he threw her rudely on the flore,
And laying both his hands upon his glave,
With dreadfull strokes let drive at him so sore,
That forst him flie abacke, himselfe to save:
Yet he therewith so felly still did rave,
That scarse the squire his hand could once upreare,
But, for advantage, ground unto him gave,
Tracing and traversing, now here, now there;
For bootlesse thing it was to think such blowes to beare.

XXIX
Whilest thus in battell they embusied were,
Belphebe, raunging in that forrest wide,
The hideous noise of their huge strokes did heare,
And drew thereto, making her eare her guide.
Whom when that theefe approching nigh espide,
With bow in hand, and arrowes ready bent,
He by his former combate would not bide,
But fled away with ghastly dreriment,
Well knowing her to be his deaths sole instrument.

XXX
Whom seeing flie, she speedily poursewed
With winged feete, as nimble as the winde,
And ever in her bow she ready shewed

The arrow to his deadly marke desynde:
As when Latonaes daughter, cruell kynde,
In vengement of her mothers great disgrace,
With fell despight her cruell arrowes tynde
Gainst wofull Niobes unhappy race,
That all the gods did mone her miserable case.

XXXI
So well she sped her and so far she ventred,
That ere unto his hellish den he raught,
Even as he ready was there to have entred,
She sent an arrow forth with mighty draught,
That in the very dore him overcaught,
And in his nape arriving, through it thrild
His greedy throte, therewith in two distraught,
That all his vitall spirites thereby spild,
And all his hairy brest with gory bloud was fild.

XXXII
Whom when on ground she groveling saw to rowle,
She ran in hast his life to have bereft:
But ere she could him reach, the sinfull sowle,
Having his carrion corse quite sencelesse left,
Was fled to hell, surcharg'd with spoile and theft.
Yet over him she there long gazing stood,
And oft admir'd his monstrous shape, and oft
His mighty limbs, whilest all with filthy bloud
The place there overflowne seemd like a sodaine flood.

XXXIII
Thenceforth she past into his dreadfull den,
Where nought but darkesome drerinesse she found,
Ne creature saw, but hearkned now and then
Some litle whispering, and soft groning sound.
With that she askt, what ghosts there under ground
Lay hid in horrour of eternall night;
And bad them, if so be they were not bound,
To come and shew themselves before the light,
Now freed from feare and danger of that dismall wight.

XXXIV
Then forth the sad Æmylia issewed,
Yet trembling every joynt through former feare;
And after her the hag, there with her mewed,
A foule and lothsome creature, did appeare;
A leman fit for such a lover deare:
That mov'd Belphebe her no lesse to hate,
Then for to rue the others heavy cheare;
Of whom she gan enquire of her estate:
Who all to her at large, as hapned, did relate.

XXXV
Thence she them brought toward the place where late
She left the gentle squire with Amoret:
There she him found by that new lovely mate,
Who lay the whiles in swoune, full sadly set,
From her faire eyes wiping the deawy wet,
Which softly stild, and kissing them atweene,
And handling soft the hurts which she did get:
For of that carle she sorely bruz'd had beene,
Als of his owne rash hand one wound was to be seene.

XXXVI
Which when she saw, with sodaine glauncing eye,
Her noble heart with sight thereof was fild
With deepe disdaine, and great indignity,
That in her wrath she thought them both have thrild
With that selfe arrow which the carle had kild:
Yet held her wrathfull hand from vengeance sore,
But drawing nigh, ere he her well beheld,
'Is this the faith?' she said,—and said no more,
But turnd her face, and fled away for evermore.

XXXVII
He, seeing her depart, arose up light,
Right sore agrieved at her sharpe reproofe,
And follow'd fast: but when he came in sight,
He durst not nigh approch, but kept aloofe,
For dread of her displeasures utmost proofe.
And evermore, when he did grace entreat,
And framed speaches fit for his behoofe,
Her mortall arrowes she at him did threat,
And forst him backe with fowle dishonor to retreat.

XXXVIII
At last, when long he follow'd had in vaine,
Yet found no ease of griefe, nor hope of grace,
Unto those woods he turned backe againe,
Full of sad anguish and in heavy case:
And finding there fit solitary place
For wofull wight, chose out a gloomy glade,
Where hardly eye mote see bright heavens face,
For mossy trees, which covered all with shade
And sad melancholy: there he his cabin made.

XXXIX
His wonted warlike weapons all he broke,
And threw away, with vow to use no more,
Ne thenceforth ever strike in battell stroke,
Ne ever word to speake to woman more;
But in that wildernesse, of men forlore,
And of the wicked world forgotten quight,

His hard mishap in dolor to deplore,
And wast his wretched daies in wofull plight;
So on him selfe to wreake his follies owne despight.

XL
And eke his garment, to be thereto meet,
He wilfully did cut and shape anew;
And his faire lockes, that wont with ointment sweet
To be embaulm'd, and sweat out dainty dew,
He let to grow and griesly to concrew,
Uncomb'd, uncurl'd, and carelesly unshed;
That in short time his face they overgrew,
And over all his shoulders did dispred,
That who he whilome was, uneath was to be red.

XLI
There he continued in this carefull plight,
Wretchedly wearing out his youthly yeares,
Through wilfull penury consumed quight,
That like a pined ghost he soone appeares.
For other food then that wilde forrest beares,
Ne other drinke there did he ever tast,
Then running water, tempred with his teares,
The more his weakened body so to wast:
That out of all mens knowledge he was worne at last.

XLII
For on a day, by fortune as it fell,
His owne deare lord, Prince Arthure, came that way,
Seeking adventures, where he mote heare tell;
And as he through the wandring wood did stray,
Having espide this cabin far away,
He to it drew, to weet who there did wonne;
Weening therein some holy hermit lay,
That did resort of sinfull people shonne;
Or else some woodman shrowded there from scorching sunne.

XLIII
Arriving there, he found this wretched man,
Spending his daies in dolour and despaire,
And through long fasting woxen pale and wan,
All overgrowen with rude and rugged haire;
That albeit his owne deare squire he were,
Yet he him knew not, ne aviz'd at all,
But like strange wight, whom he had seene no where,
Saluting him, gan into speach to fall,
And pitty much his plight, that liv'd like outcast thrall.

XLIV
But to his speach he aunswered no whit,
But stood still mute, as if he had beene dum,

Ne signe of sence did shew, ne common wit,
As one with griefe and anguishe overcum,
And unto every thing did aunswere mum:
And ever when the Prince unto him spake,
He louted lowly, as did him becum,
And humble homage did unto him make,
Midst sorrow shewing joyous semblance for his sake.

XLV
At which his uncouth guise and usage quaint
The Prince did wonder much, yet could not ghesse
The cause of that his sorrowfull constraint;
Yet weend by secret signes of manlinesse,
Which close appeard in that rude brutishnesse,
That he whilome some gentle swaine had beene,
Traind up in feats of armes and knightlinesse;
Which he observ'd, by that he him had seene
To weld his naked sword, and try the edges keene;

XLVI
And eke by that he saw on every tree
How he the name of one engraven had,
Which likly was his liefest love to be,
For whom he now so sorely was bestad;
Which was by him BELPHEBE rightly rad.
Yet who was that Belphebe he ne wist;
Yet saw he often how he wexed glad,
When he it heard, and how the ground he kist,
Wherein it written was, and how himselfe he blist.

XLVII
Tho, when he long had marked his demeanor,
And saw that all he said and did was vaine,
Ne ought mote make him change his wonted tenor,
Ne ought mote ease or mitigate his paine,
He left him there in languor to remaine,
Till time for him should remedy provide,
And him restore to former grace againe.
Which for it is too long here to abide,
I will deferre the end untill another tide.

CANTO VIII

The gentle squire recovers grace:
Sclaunder her guests doth staine:
Corflambo chaseth Placidas,
And is by Arthure slaine.

I
Well said the wiseman, now prov'd true by this,
Which to this gentle squire did happen late,
That the displeasure of the mighty is
Then death it selfe more dread and desperate.
For naught the same may calme ne mitigate,
Till time the tempest doe thereof delay
With sufferaunce soft, which rigour can abate,
And have the sterne remembrance wypt away
Of bitter thoughts, which deepe therein infixed lay.

II
Like as it fell to this unhappy boy,
Whose tender heart the faire Belphebe had
With one sterne looke so daunted, that no joy
In all his life, which afterwards he lad,
He ever tasted; but with penaunce sad
And pensive sorrow pind and wore away,
Ne ever laught, ne once shew'd countenance glad;
But alwaies wept and wailed night and day,
As blasted bloosme through heat doth languish and decay.

III
Till on a day, as in his wonted wise
His doole he made, there chaunst a turtle dove
To come where he his dolors did devise,
That likewise late had lost her dearest love,
Which losse her made like passion also prove.
Who seeing his sad plight, her tender heart
With deare compassion deeply did emmove,
That she gan mone his undeserved smart,
And with her dolefull accent beare with him a part.

IV
Shee sitting by him, as on ground he lay,
Her mournefull notes full piteously did frame,
And thereof made a lamentable lay,
So sensibly compyld, that in the same
Him seemed oft he heard his owne right name.
With that he forth would poure so plenteous teares,
And beat his breast unworthy of such blame,
And knocke his head, and rend his rugged heares,
That could have perst the hearts of tigres and of beares.

V
Thus, long this gentle bird to him did use
Withouten dread of perill to repaire
Unto his wonne, and with her mournefull muse
Him to recomfort in his greatest care,
That much did ease his mourning and misfare:

And every day, for guerdon of her song,
He part of his small feast to her would share;
That, at the last, of all his woe and wrong
Companion she became, and so continued long.

VI
Upon a day, as she him sate beside,
By chance he certaine miniments forth drew,
Which yet with him as relickes did abide
Of all the bounty which Belphebe threw
On him, whilst goodly grace she did him shew:
Amongst the rest a jewell rich he found,
That was a ruby of right perfect hew,
Shap'd like a heart yet bleeding of the wound,
And with a litle golden chaine about it bound.

VII
The same he tooke, and with a riband new,
In which his ladies colours were, did bind
About the turtles necke, that with the vew
Did greatly solace his engrieved mind.
All unawares the bird, when she did find
Her selfe so deckt, her nimble wings displaid,
And flew away, as lightly as the wind:
Which sodaine accident him much dismaid,
And looking after long, did marke which way she straid.

VIII
But when as long he looked had in vaine,
Yet saw her forward still to make her flight,
His weary eie returnd to him againe,
Full of discomfort and disquiet plight,
That both his juell he had lost so light,
And eke his deare companion of his care.
But that sweet bird departing flew forth right
Through the wide region of the wastfull aire,
Untill she came where wonned his Belphebe faire.

IX
There found she her (as then it did betide)
Sitting in covert shade of arbors sweet,
After late weary toile, which she had tride
In salvage chase, to rest as seem'd her meet.
There she alighting, fell before her feet,
And gan to her her mournful plaint to make,
As was her wont, thinking to let her weet
The great tormenting griefe that for her sake
Her gentle squire through her displeasure did pertake.

X
She her beholding with attentive eye,

At length did marke about her purple brest
That precious juell, which she formerly
Had knowne right well, with colourd ribbands drest:
Therewith she rose in hast, and her addrest
With ready hand it to have reft away:
But the swift bird obayd not her behest,
But swarv'd aside, and there againe did stay;
She follow'd her, and thought againe it to assay.

XI
And ever when she nigh approcht, the dove
Would flit a litle forward, and then stay,
Till she drew neare, and then againe remove;
So tempting her still to pursue the pray,
And still from her escaping soft away:
Till that at length into that forrest wide
She drew her far, and led with slow delay.
In th' end she her unto that place did guide,
Whereas that wofull man in languor did abide.

XII
Eftsoones she flew unto his fearelesse hand,
And there a piteous ditty new deviz'd,
As if she would have made her understand
His sorrowes cause, to be of her despis'd.
Whom when she saw in wretched weedes disguiz'd,
With heary glib deform'd, and meiger face,
Like ghost late risen from his grave agryz'd,
She knew him not, but pittied much his case,
And wisht it were in her to doe him any grace.

XIII
He her beholding, at her feet downe fell,
And kist the ground on which her sole did tread,
And washt the same with water, which did well
From his moist eies, and like two streames procead;
Yet spake no word whereby she might aread
What mister wight he was, or what he ment;
But as one daunted with her presence dread,
Onely few ruefull lookes unto her sent,
As messengers of his true meaning and intent.

XIV
Yet nathemore his meaning she ared,
But wondred much at his so selcouth case,
And by his persons secret seemlyhed
Well weend that he had beene some man of place,
Before misfortune did his hew deface:
That, being mov'd with ruth, she thus bespake:
'Ah, wofull man! what Heavens hard disgrace,
Or wrath of cruell wight on thee ywrake,

Or selfe disliked life, doth thee thus wretched make?

XV
'If Heaven, then none may it redresse or blame,
Sith to his powre we all are subject borne;
If wrathfull wight, then fowle rebuke and shame
Be theirs, that have so cruell thee forlorne;
But if through inward griefe or wilfull scorne
Of life it be, then better doe advise;
For he whose daies in wilfull woe are worne,
The grace of his Creator doth despise,
That will not use his gifts for thanklesse nigardise.'

XVI
When so he heard her say, eftsoones he brake
His sodaine silence, which he long had pent,
And sighing inly deepe, her thus bespake:
'Then have they all themselves against me bent:
For Heaven, first author of my languishment,
Envying my too great felicity,
Did closely with a cruell one consent
To cloud my daies in dolefull misery,
And make me loath this life, still longing for to die.

XVII
'Ne any but your selfe, O dearest dred,
Hath done this wrong, to wreake on worthlesse wight
Your high displesure, through misdeeming bred:
That, when your pleasure is to deeme aright,
Ye may redresse, and me restore to light.'
Which sory words her mightie hart did mate
With mild regard, to see his ruefull plight,
That her inburning wrath she gan abate,
And him receiv'd againe to former favours state.

XVIII
In which he long time afterwards did lead
An happie life with grace and good accord,
Fearlesse of fortunes chaunge or envies dread,
And eke all mindlesse of his owne deare lord,
The noble Prince, who never heard one word
Of tydings, what did unto him betide,
Or what good fortune did to him afford,
But through the endlesse world did wander wide,
Him seeking evermore, yet no where him descride.

XIX
Till on a day, as through that wood he rode,
He chaunst to come where those two ladies late,
Æmylia and Amoret, abode,
Both in full sad and sorrowfull estate;

The one right feeble through the evill rate
Of food, which in her duresse she had found:
The other almost dead and desperate
Through her late hurts, and through that haplesse wound
With which the squire in her defence her sore astound.

XX
Whom when the Prince beheld, he gan to rew
The evill case in which those ladies lay;
But most was moved at the piteous vew,
Of Amoret, so neare unto decay,
That her great daunger did him much dismay.
Eftsoones that pretious liquour forth he drew,
Which he in store about him kept alway,
And with few drops thereof did softly dew
Her wounds, that unto strength restor'd her soone anew.

XXI
Tho, when they both recovered were right well,
He gan of them inquire, what evill guide
Them thether brought, and how their harmes befell.
To whom they told all that did them betide,
And how from thraldome vile they were untide
Of that same wicked carle, by virgins hond;
Whose bloudie corse they shew'd him there beside,
And eke his cave, in which they both were bond:
At which he wondred much, when all those signes he fond.

XXII
And evermore he greatly did desire
To know, what virgin did them thence unbind;
And oft of them did earnestly inquire,
Where was her won, and how he mote her find.
But when as nought according to his mind
He could outlearne, he them from ground did reare,
(No service lothsome to a gentle kind)
And on his warlike beast them both did beare,
Himselfe by them on foot, to succour them from feare.

XXIII
So when that forrest they had passed well,
A litle cotage farre away they spide,
To which they drew, ere night upon them fell;
And entring in, found none therein abide,
But one old woman sitting there beside,
Upon the ground, in ragged rude attyre,
With filthy lockes about her scattered wide,
Gnawing her nayles for felnesse and for yre,
And there out sucking venime to her parts entyre.

XXIV

A foule and loathly creature sure in sight,
And in conditions to be loath'd no lesse:
For she was stuft with rancour and despight
Up to the throat; that oft with bitternesse
It forth would breake, and gush in great excesse,
Pouring out streames of poyson and of gall
Gainst all that truth or vertue doe professe;
Whom she with leasings lewdly did miscall,
And wickedly backbite: her name men Sclaunder call.

XXV
Her nature is, all goodnesse to abuse,
And causelesse crimes continually to frame,
With which she guiltlesse persons may accuse,
And steale away the crowne of their good name;
Ne ever knight so bold, ne ever dame
So chast and loyall liv'd, but she would strive
With forged cause them falsely to defame;
Ne ever thing so well was doen alive,
But she with blame would blot, and of due praise deprive.

XXVI
Her words were not, as common words are ment,
T' expresse the meaning of the inward mind,
But noysome breath, and poysnous spirit sent
From inward parts, with cancred malice lind,
And breathed forth with blast of bitter wind;
Which passing through the eares would pierce the hart,
And wound the soule it selfe with griefe unkind:
For like the stings of aspes, that kill with smart,
Her spightfull words did pricke and wound the inner part.

XXVII
Such was that hag, unmeet to host such guests,
Whom greatest princes court would welcome fayne;
But neede, that answers not to all requests,
Bad them not looke for better entertayne;
And eke that age despysed nicenesse vaine,
Enur'd to hardnesse and to homely fare,
Which them to warlike discipline did trayne,
And manly limbs endur'd with litle care
Against all hard mishaps and fortunelesse misfare.

XXVIII
Then all that evening, welcomed with cold
And chearelesse hunger, they together spent;
Yet found no fault, but that the hag did scold
And rayle at them with grudgefull discontent,
For lodging there without her owne consent:
Yet they endured all with patience milde,
And unto rest themselves all onely lent;

Regardlesse, of that queane so base and vilde
To be unjustly blamd, and bitterly revilde.

XXIX
Here well I weene, when as these rimes be red
With misregard, that some rash witted wight,
Whose looser thought will lightly be misled,
These gentle ladies will misdeeme too light,
For thus conversing with this noble knight;
Sith now of dayes such temperance is rare
And hard to finde, that heat of youthfull spright
For ought will from his greedie pleasure spare:
More hard for hungry steed t' abstaine from pleasant lare.

XXX
But antique age, yet in the infancie
Of time, did live then like an innocent,
In simple truth and blamelesse chastitie,
Ne then of guile had made experiment,
But voide of vile and treacherous intent,
Held vertue for it selfe in soveraine awe:
Then loyall love had royall regiment,
And each unto his lust did make a lawe,
From all forbidden things his liking to withdraw.

XXXI
The lyon there did with the lambe consort,
And eke the dove sate by the faulcons side,
Ne each of other feared fraud or tort,
But did in safe securitie abide,
Withouten perill of the stronger pride:
But when the world woxe old, it woxe warre old
(Whereof it hight) and having shortly tride
The traines of wit, in wickednesse woxe bold,
And dared of all sinnes the secrets to unfold.

XXXII
Then beautie, which was made to represent
The great Creatours owne resemblance bright,
Unto abuse of lawlesse lust was lent,
And made the baite of bestiall delight:
Then faire grew foule, and foule grew faire in sight,
And that which wont to vanquish God and man
Was made the vassall of the victors might;
Then did her glorious flowre wex dead and wan,
Despisd and troden downe of all that overran.

XXXIII
And now it is so utterly decayd,
That any bud thereof doth scarse remaine,
But if few plants, preserv'd through heavenly ayd,

In princes court doe hap to sprout against,
Dew'd with her drops of bounties soveraine,
Which from that goodly glorious flowre proceed,
Sprung of the auncient stocke of princes straine,
Now th' onely remnant of that royall breed,
Whose noble kind at first was sure of heavenly seed.

XXXIV
Tho, soone as day discovered heavens face
To sinfull men with darknes overdight,
This gentle crew gan from their eye-lids chace
The drowzie humour of the dampish night,
And did themselves unto their journey dight.
So forth they yode, and forward softly paced,
That them to view had bene an uncouth sight,
How all the way the Prince on footpace traced,
The ladies both on horse, together fast embraced.

XXXV
Soone as they thence departed were afore,
That shamefull hag, the slaunder of her sexe,
Them follow'd fast, and them reviled sore,
Him calling theefe, them whores; that much did vexe
His noble hart: thereto she did annexe
False crimes and facts, such as they never ment,
That those two ladies much asham'd did wexe:
The more did she pursue her lewd intent,
And rayl'd and rag'd, till she had all her poyson spent.

XXXVI
At last, when they were passed out of sight,
Yet she did not her spightful speach forbeare,
But after them did barke, and still back-bite,
Though there were none her hatefull words to heare:
Like as a curre doth felly bite and teare
The stone which passed straunger at him threw;
So she them seeing past the reach of eare,
Against the stones and trees did rayle anew,
Till she had duld the sting which in her tongs end grew.

XXXVII
They, passing forth, kept on their readie way,
With easie steps so soft as foot could stryde,
Both for great feeblesse, which did oft assay
Faire Amoret, that scarcely she could ryde,
And eke through heavie armes, which sore annoyd
The Prince on foot, not wonted so to fare;
Whose steadie hand was faine his steede to guyde,
And all the way from trotting hard to spare;
So was his toyle the more, the more that was his care.

XXXVIII
At length they spide where towards them with speed
A squire came gallopping, as he would flie,
Bearing a little dwarfe before his steed,
That all the way full loud for aide did crie,
That seem'd his shrikes would rend the brasen skie:
Whom after did a mightie man pursew,
Ryding upon a dromedare on hie,
Of stature huge, and horrible of hew,
That would have maz'd a man his dreadfull face to vew.

XXXIX
For from his fearefull eyes two fierie beames,
More sharpe then points of needles, did proceede,
Shooting forth farre away two flaming streames,
Full of sad powre, that poysonous bale did breede
To all that on him lookt without good heed,
And secretly his enemies did slay:
Like as the basiliske, of serpents seede,
From powrefull eyes close venim doth convay
Into the lookers hart, and killeth farre away.

XL
He all the way did rage at that same squire,
And after him full many threatnings threw,
With curses vaine in his avengefull ire:
But none of them (so fast away he flew)
Him overtooke before he came in vew.
Where when he saw the Prince in armour bright,
He cald to him aloud, his case to rew,
And rescue him through succour of his might,
From that his cruell foe, that him pursewd in sight.

XLI
Eftsoones the Prince tooke downe those ladies twaine
From loftie steede, and mounting in their stead,
Came to that squire, yet trembling every vaine:
Of whom he gan enquire his cause of dread:
Who as he gan the same to him aread,
Loe! hard behind his backe his foe was prest,
With dreadfull weapon aymed at his head,
That unto death had doen him unredrest,
Had not the noble Prince his readie stroke represt.

XLII
Who, thrusting boldly twixt him and the blow,
The burden of the deadly brunt did beare
Upon his shield, which lightly he did throw
Over his head, before the harme came neare.
Nathlesse it fell with so despiteous dreare
And heavie sway, that hard unto his crowne

The shield it drove, and did the covering reare:
Therewith both squire and dwarfe did tomble downe
Unto the earth, and lay long while in senselesse swowne.

XLIII
Whereat the Prince full wrath, his strong right hand
In full avengement heaved up on hie,
And stroke the Pagan with his steely brand
So sore, that to his saddle bow thereby
He bowed low, and so a while did lie:
And sure, had not his massie yron mace
Betwixt him and his hurt bene happily,
It would have cleft him to the girding place;
Yet, as it was, it did astonish him long space.

XLIV
But when he to himselfe returnd againe,
All full of rage he gan to curse and sweare,
And vow by Mahoune that he should be slaine.
With that his murdrous mace he up did reare,
That seemed nought the souse thereof could beare,
And therewith smote at him with all his might.
But ere that it to him approched neare,
The royall child, with readie quicke foresight,
Did shun the proofe thereof and it avoyded light.

XLV
But ere his hand he could recure againe,
To ward his bodie from the balefull stound,
He smote at him with all his might and maine,
So furiously, that, ere he wist, he found
His head before him tombling on the ground.
The whiles his babling tongue did yet blaspheme
And curse his god, that did him so confound;
The whiles his life ran foorth in bloudie streame,
His soule descended downe into the Stygian reame.

XLVI
Which when that squire beheld, he woxe full glad
To see his foe breath out his spright in vaine:
But that same dwarfe right sorie seem'd and sad,
And howld aloud to see his lord there slaine,
And rent his haire and scratcht his face for paine.
Then gan the Prince at leasure to inquire
Of all the accident, there hapned plaine,
And what he was, whose eyes did flame with fire;
All which was, thus to him declared by that squire.

XLVII
'This mightie man,' quoth he, 'whom you have slaine,
Of an huge geauntesse whylome was bred;

And by his strength rule to himselfe did gaine
Of many nations into thraldome led,
And mightie kingdomes of his force adred;
Whom yet he conquer'd not by bloudie fight,
Ne hostes of men with banners brode dispred,
But by the powre of his infectious sight,
With which he killed all that came within his might.

XLVIII
'Ne was he ever vanquished afore,
But ever vanquisht all with whom he fought;
Ne was there man so strong, but he downe bore,
Ne woman yet so faire, but he her brought
Unto his bay, and captived her thought.
For most of strength and beautie his desire
Was spoyle to make, and wast them unto nought,
By casting secret flakes of lustfull fire
From his false eyes, into their harts and parts entire.

XLIX
'Therefore Corflambo was he cald aright,
Though namelesse there his bodie now doth lie;
Yet hath he left one daughter that is hight
The faire Pœana; who seemes outwardly
So faire as ever yet saw living eie:
And were her vertue like her beautie bright,
She were as faire as any under skie.
But ah! she given is to vaine delight,
And eke too loose of life, and eke of love too light.

L
'So as it fell, there was a gentle squire,
That lov'd a ladie of high parentage;
But for his meane degree might not aspire
To match so high, her friends with counsell sage
Dissuaded her from such a disparage.
But she, whose hart to love was wholly lent,
Out of his hands could not redeeme her gage,
But firmely following her first intent,
Resolv'd with him to wend, gainst all her friends consent.

LI
'So twixt themselves they pointed time and place,
To which when he according did repaire,
An hard mishap and disaventrous case
Him chaunst; in stead of his Æmylia faire,
This gyants sonne, that lies there on the laire
An headlesse heape, him unawares there caught,
And, all dismayd through mercilesse despaire,
Him wretched thrall unto his dongeon brought,
Where he remaines, of all unsuccour'd and unsought.

LII
'This gyants daughter came upon a day
Unto the prison in her joyous glee,
To view the thrals which there in bondage lay:
Amongst the rest she chaunced there to see
This lovely swaine, the squire of low degree;
To whom she did her liking lightly cast,
And wooed him her paramour to bee:
From day to day she woo'd and prayd him fast,
And for his love him promist libertie at last.

LIII
'He, though affide unto a former love,
To whom his faith he firmely ment to hold,
Yet seeing not how thence he mote remove,
But by that meanes which fortune did unfold,
Her graunted love, but with affection cold,
To win her grace his libertie to get.
Yet she him still detaines in captive hold,
Fearing least, if she should him freely set,
He would her shortly leave, and former love forget.

LIV
'Yet so much favour she to him hath hight
Above the rest, that he sometimes may space
And walke about her gardens of delight,
Having a keeper still with him in place;
Which keeper is this dwarfe, her dearling base,
To whom the keyes of every prison dore
By her committed be, of speciall grace,
And at his will may whom he list restore,
And whom he list reserve, to be afflicted more.

LV
'Whereof when tydings came unto mine eare,
Full inly sorie, for the fervent zeale
Which I to him as to my soule did beare,
I thether went; where I did long conceale
My selfe, till that the dwarfe did me reveale,
And told his dame her squire of low degree
Did secretly out of her prison steale;
For me he did mistake that squire to bee;
For never two so like did living creature see.

LVI
'Then was I taken and before her brought:
Who, through the likenesse of my outward hew,
Being likewise beguiled in her thought,
Gan blame me much for being so untrew,
To seeke by flight her fellowship t' eschew,

That lov'd me deare, as dearest thing alive.
Thence she commaunded me to prison new;
Whereof I glad did not gainesay nor strive,
But suffred that same dwarfe me to her dongeon drive.

LVII
'There did I finde mine onely faithfull frend
In heavy plight and sad perplexitie;
Whereof I sorie, yet my selfe did bend
Him to recomfort with my companie.
But him the more agreev'd I found thereby:
For all his joy, he said, in that distresse,
Was mine and his Æmylias libertie.
Æmylia well he lov'd, as I mote ghesse;
Yet greater love to me then her he did professe.

LVIII
'But I with better reason him aviz'd,
And shew'd him how, through error and mis-thought
Of our like persons, eath to be disguiz'd,
Or his exchange or freedome might be wrought.
Whereto full loth was he, ne would for ought
Consent that I, who stood all fearelesse free,
Should wilfully be into thraldome brought,
Till Fortune did perforce it so decree.
Yet, overrul'd at last, he did to me agree.

LIX
'The morrow next, about the wonted howre,
The dwarfe cald at the doore of Amyas,
To come forthwith unto his ladies bowre.
In steed of whom forth came I, Placidas,
And undiscerned forth with him did pas.
There with great joyance and with gladsome glee
Of faire Pœana I received was,
And oft imbrast, as if that I were hee,
And with kind words accoyd, vowing great love to mee.

LX
'Which I, that was not bent to former love,
As was my friend, that had her long refusd,
Did well accept, as well it did behove,
And to the present neede it wisely usd.
My former hardnesse first I faire excusd;
And after promist large amends to make.
With such smooth termes her error I abusd,
To my friends good more then for mine owne sake,
For whose sole libertie I love and life did stake.

LXI
'Thenceforth I found more favour at her hand,

That to her dwarfe, which had me in his charge,
She bad to lighten my too heavie band,
And graunt more scope to me to walke at large.
So on a day, as by the flowrie marge
Of a fresh streame I with that elfe did play,
Finding no meanes how I might us enlarge,
But if that dwarfe I could with me convay,
I lightly snatcht him up, and with me bore away.

LXII
'Thereat he shriekt aloud, that with his cry
The tyrant selfe came forth with yelling bray,
And me pursew'd; but nathemore would I
Forgoe the purchase of my gotten pray,
But have perforce him hether brought away.'
Thus as they talked, loe! where nigh at hand
Those ladies two, yet doubtfull through dismay,
In presence came, desirous t' understand
Tydings of all which there had hapned on the land.

LXIII
Where soone as sad Æmylia did espie
Her captive lovers friend, young Placidas,
All mindlesse of her wonted modestie,
She to him ran, and him with streight embras
Enfolding said: 'And lives yet Amyas?'
'He lives,' quoth he, 'and his Æmylia loves.'
'Then lesse,' said she, 'by all the woe I pas,
With which my weaker patience Fortune proves.
But what mishap thus long him fro my selfe removes?'

LXIV
Then gan he all this storie to renew,
And tell the course of his captivitie;
That her deare hart full deepely made to rew,
And sigh full sore, to heare the miserie,
In which so long he mercilesse did lie.
Then, after many teares and sorrowes spent,
She deare besought the Prince of remedie:
Who thereto did with readie will consent,
And well perform'd, as shall appeare by his event.

CANTO IX

The squire of low degree, releast,
Pœana takes to wife:
Britomart fightes with many knights;
Prince Arthur stints their strife.

I

Hard is the doubt, and difficult to deeme,
When all three kinds of love together meet,
And doe dispart the hart with powre extreme,
Whether shall weigh the balance downe; to weet,
The deare affection unto kindred sweet,
Or raging fire of love to woman kind,
Or zeale of friends combynd with vertues meet.
But of them all, the band of vertuous mind,
Me seemes, the gentle hart should most assured bind.

II

For naturall affection soone doth cesse,
And quenched is with Cupids greater flame:
But faithfull friendship doth them both suppresse,
And them with maystring discipline doth tame,
Through thoughts aspyring to eternall fame.
For as the soule doth rule the earthly masse,
And all the service of the bodie frame,
So love of soule doth love of bodie passe,
No lesse then perfect gold surmounts the meanest brasse.

III

All which who list by tryall to assay,
Shall in this storie find approved plaine;
In which these squires true friendship more did sway,
Then either care of parents could refraine,
Or love of fairest ladie could constraine.
For though Pœana were as faire as morne,
Yet did this trustie squire with proud disdaine
For his friends sake her offred favours scorne,
And she her selfe her syre, of whom she was yborne.

IV

Now after that Prince Arthur graunted had
To yeeld strong succour to that gentle swayne,
Who now long time had lyen in prison sad,
He gan advise how best he mote darrayne
That enterprize, for greatest glories gayne.
That headlesse tyrants tronke he reard from ground,
And having ympt the head to it agayne,
Upon his usuall beast it firmely bound,
And made it so to ride as it alive was found.

V

Then did he take that chaced squire, and layd
Before the ryder, as he captive were,
And made his dwarfe, though with unwilling ayd,
To guide the beast that did his maister beare,

Till to his castle they approched neare.
Whom when the watch, that kept continuall ward,
Saw comming home, all voide of doubtfull feare,
He, running downe, the gate to him unbard;
Whom straight the Prince ensuing, in together far'd.

VI
There he did find in her delitious boure
The faire Pœana playing on a rote,
Complayning of her cruell paramoure,
And singing all her sorrow to the note,
As she had learned readily by rote;
That with the sweetnesse of her rare delight
The Prince halfe rapt, began on her to dote:
Till, better him bethinking of the right,
He her unwares attacht, and captive held by might.

VII
Whence being forth produc'd, when she perceived
Her owne deare sire, she cald to him for aide.
But when of him no aunswere she received,
But saw him sencelesse by the squire upstaide,
She weened well that then she was betraide:
Then gan she loudly cry, and weepe, and waile,
And that same squire of treason to upbraide:
But all in vaine; her plaints might not prevaile;
Ne none there was to reskue her, ne none to baile.

VIII
Then tooke he that same dwarfe, and him compeld
To open unto him the prison dore,
And forth to bring those thrals which there he held.
Thence forth were brought to him above a score
Of knights and squires to him unknowne afore:
All which he did from bitter bondage free,
And unto former liberty restore.
Amongst the rest, that squire of low degree
Came forth full weake and wan, not like him selfe to bee.

IX
Whom soone as faire Æmylia beheld,
And Placidas, they both unto him ran,
And him embracing fast betwixt them held,
Striving to comfort him all that they can,
And kissing oft his visage pale and wan;
That faire Pæana, them beholding both,
Gan both envy, and bitterly to ban;
Through jealous passion weeping inly wroth,
To see the sight perforce, that both her eyes were loth.

X

But when a while they had together beene,
And diversly conferred of their case,
She, though full oft she both of them had seene
A sunder, yet not ever in one place,
Began to doubt, when she them saw embrace,
Which was the captive squire she lov'd so deare,
Deceived through great likenesse of their face,
For they so like in person did appeare,
That she uneath discerned, whether whether weare.

XI
And eke the Prince, when as he them avized,
Their like resemblaunce much admired there,
And mazd how Nature had so well disguized
Her worke, and counterfet her selfe so nere,
As if that by one patterne seene somewhere
She had them made a paragone to be,
Or whether it through skill or errour were.
Thus gazing long, at them much wondred he;
So did the other knights and squires, which them did see.

XII
Then gan they ransacke that same castle strong,
In which he found great store of hoorded threasure,
The which that tyrant gathered had by wrong
And tortious powre, without respect or measure.
Upon all which the Briton Prince made seasure,
And afterwards continu'd there a while,
To rest him selfe, and solace in soft pleasure
Those weaker ladies after weary toile;
To whom he did divide part of his purchast spoile.

XIII
And for more joy, that captive lady faire,
The faire Pæana, he enlarged free,
And by the rest did set in sumptuous chaire,
To feast and frollicke; nathemore would she
Shew gladsome countenaunce nor pleasaunt glee,
But grieved was for losse both of her sire,
And eke of lordship, with both land and fee:
But most she touched was with griefe entire
For losse of her new love, the hope of her desire.

XIV
But her the Prince, through his well wonted grace,
To better termes of myldnesse did entreat
From that fowle rudenesse which did her deface;
And that same bitter corsive, which did eat
Her tender heart, and made refraine from meat,
He with good thewes and speaches well applyde
Did mollifie, and calme her raging heat.

For though she were most faire, and goodly dyde,
Yet she it all did mar with cruelty and pride.

XV
And for to shut up all in friendly love,
Sith love was first the ground of all her griefe,
That trusty squire he wisely well did move
Not to despise that dame, which lov'd him liefe,
Till he had made of her some better priefe,
But to accept her to his wedded wife.
Thereto he offred for to make him chiefe
Of all her land and lordship during life:
He yeelded, and her tooke; so stinted all their strife.

XVI
From that day forth in peace and joyous blis
They liv'd together long without debate,
Ne private jarre, ne spite of enemis
Could shake the safe assuraunce of their state.
And she, whom Nature did so faire create
That she mote match the fairest of her daies,
Yet with lewd loves and lust intemperate
Had it defaste, thenceforth reformd her waies,
That all men much admyrde her change, and spake her praise.

XVII
Thus when the Prince had perfectly compylde
These paires of friends in peace and setled rest,
Him selfe, whose minde did travell as with chylde
Of his old love, conceav'd in secret brest,
Resolved to pursue his former quest;
And taking leave of all, with him did beare
Faire Amoret, whom Fortune by bequest
Had left in his protection whileare,
Exchanged out of one into an other feare.

XVIII
Feare of her safety did her not constraine,
For well she wist now in a mighty hond
Her person, late in perill, did remaine,
Who able was all daungers to withstond:
But now in feare of shame she more did stond,
Seeing her selfe all soly succourlesse,
Left in the victors powre, like vassall bond;
Whose will her weakenesse could no way represse,
In case his burning lust should breake into excesse.

XIX
But cause of feare sure had she none at all
Of him, who goodly learned had of yore
The course of loose affection to forstall,

And lawlesse lust to rule with reasons lore;
That all the while he by his side her bore,
She was as safe as in a sanctuary.
Thus many miles they two together wore,
To seeke their loves dispersed diversly,
Yet neither shewed to other their hearts privity.

XX
At length they came, whereas a troupe of knights
They saw together skirmishing, as seemed:
Sixe they were all, all full of fell despight,
But foure of them the battell best beseemed,
That which of them was best mote not be deemed.
Those foure were they from whom false Florimell
By Braggadochio lately was redeemed;
To weet, sterne Druon, and lewd Claribell,
Love-lavish Blandamour, and lustfull Paridell.

XXI
Druons delight was all in single life,
And unto ladies love would lend no leasure:
The more was Claribell enraged rife
With fervent flames, and loved out of measure:
So eke lov'd Blandamour, but yet at pleasure
Would change his liking, and new lemans prove:
But Paridell of love did make no threasure,
But lusted after all that him did move.
So diversly these foure disposed were to love.

XXII
But those two other, which beside them stoode,
Were Britomart and gentle Scudamour;
Who all the while beheld their wrathfull moode,
And wondred at their impacable stoure,
Whose like they never saw till that same houre:
So dreadfull strokes each did at other drive,
And laid on load with all their might and powre,
As if that every dint the ghost would rive
Out of their wretched corses, and their lives deprive.

XXIII
As when Dan Æolus, in great displeasure,
For losse of his deare love by Neptune hent,
Sends forth the winds out of his hidden threasure,
Upon the sea to wreake his fell intent;
They, breaking forth with rude unruliment
From all foure parts of heaven, doe rage full sore,
And tosse the deepes, and teare the firmament,
And all the world confound with wide uprore,
As if in stead thereof they Chaos would restore.

XXIV
Cause of their discord and so fell debate
Was for the love of that same snowy maid,
Whome they had lost in turneyment of late,
And seeking long, to weet which way she straid,
Met here together, where, through lewd upbraide
Of Ate and Duessa, they fell out,
And each one taking part in others aide,
This cruell conflict raised thereabout,
Whose dangerous successe depended yet in dout.

XXV
For sometimes Paridell and Blandamour
The better had, and bet the others backe;
Eftsoones the others did the field recoure,
And on their foes did worke full cruell wracke:
Yet neither would their fiendlike fury slacke,
But evermore their malice did augment;
Till that uneath they forced were, for lacke
Of breath, their raging rigour to relent,
And rest themselves for to recover spirits spent.

XXVI
Then gan they change their sides, and new parts take;
For Paridell did take to Druons side,
For old despight, which now forth newly brake
Gainst Blandamour, whom alwaies he envide;
And Blandamour to Claribell relide:
So all afresh gan former fight renew.
As when two barkes, this caried with the tide,
That with the wind, contrary courses sew,
If wind and tide doe change, their courses change anew.

XXVII
Thenceforth they much more furiously gan fare,
As if but then the battell had begonne,
Ne helmets bright ne hawberks strong did spare,
That through the clifts the vermeil bloud out sponne,
And all adowne their riven sides did ronne.
Such mortall malice wonder was to see
In friends profest, and so great outrage donne:
But sooth is said, and tride in each degree,
Faint friends when they fall out most cruell fomen bee.

XXVIII
Thus they long while continued in fight,
Till Scudamour and that same Briton maide
By fortune in that place did chance to light:
Whom soone as they with wrathfull eie bewraide,
They gan remember of the fowle upbraide,
The which that Britonesse had to them donne,

In that late turney for the snowy maide;
Where she had them both shamefully fordonne,
And eke the famous prize of beauty from them wonne.

XXIX
Eftsoones all burning with a fresh desire
Of fell revenge, in their malicious mood
They from them selves gan turne their furious ire,
And cruell blades, yet steeming with whot bloud,
Against those two let drive, as they were wood:
Who wondring much at that so sodaine fit,
Yet nought dismayd, them stoutly well withstood;
Ne yeelded foote, ne once abacke did flit,
But being doubly smitten, likewise doubly smit.

XXX
The warlike dame was on her part assaid
Of Claribell and Blandamour attone;
And Paridell and Druon fiercely laid
At Scudamour, both his professed fone.
Foure charged two, and two surcharged one;
Yet did those two them selves so bravely beare,
That the other litle gained by the lone,
But with their owne repayed duely weare,
And usury withall: such gaine was gotten deare.

XXXI
Full oftentimes did Britomart assay
To speake to them, and some emparlance move;
But they for nought their cruell hands would stay,
Ne lend an eare to ought that might behove:
As when an eager mastiffe once doth prove
The tast of bloud of some engored beast,
No words may rate, nor rigour him remove
From greedy hold of that his blouddy feast:
So litle did they hearken to her sweet beheast.

XXXII
Whom when the Briton Prince a farre beheld
With ods of so unequall match opprest,
His mighty heart with indignation sweld,
And inward grudge fild his heroicke brest:
Eftsoones him selfe he to their aide addrest,
And thrusting fierce into the thickest preace,
Divided them, how ever loth to rest,
And would them faine from battell to surceasse,
With gentle words perswading them to friendly peace.

XXXIII
But they so farre from peace or patience were,
That all at once at him gan fiercely flie,

And lay on load, as they him downe would beare:
Like to a storme, which hovers under skie,
Long here and there and round about doth stie,
At length breakes downe in raine, and haile, and sleet,
First from one coast, till nought thereof be drie;
And then another, till that likewise fleet;
And so from side to side till all the world it weet.

XXXIV
But now their forces greatly were decayd,
The Prince yet being fresh untoucht afore;
Who them with speaches milde gan first disswade
From such foule outrage, and them long forbore:
Till, seeing them through suffrance hartned more,
Him selfe he bent their furies to abate,
And layd at them so sharpely and so sore,
That shortly them compelled to retrate,
And being brought in daunger, to relent too late.

XXXV
But now his courage being throughly fired,
He ment to make them know their follies prise,
Had not those two him instantly desired
T' asswage his wrath, and pardon their mesprise.
At whose request he gan him selfe advise
To stay his hand, and of a truce to treat
In milder tearmes, as list them to devise:
Mongst which, the cause of their so cruell heat
He did them aske: who all that passed gan repeat;

XXXVI
And told at large how that same errant knight,
To weet, faire Britomart, them late had foyled
In open turney, and by wrongfull fight
Both of their publicke praise had them despoyled,
And also of their private loves beguyled;
Of two full hard to read the harder theft.
But she that wrongfull challenge soone assoyled,
And shew'd that she had not that lady reft,
(As they supposd) but her had to her liking left.

XXXVII
To whom the Prince thus goodly well replied:
'Certes, sir knights, ye seemen much to blame,
To rip up wrong that battell once hath tried;
Wherein the honor both of armes ye shame,
And eke the love of ladies foule defame;
To whom the world this franchise ever yeelded,
That of their loves choise they might freedom clame,
And in that right should by all knights be shielded:
Gainst which, me seemes, this war ye wrongfully have wielded.'

XXXVIII
'And yet,' quoth she, 'a greater wrong remaines:
For I thereby my former love have lost,
Whom seeking ever since, with endlesse paines,
Hath me much sorrow and much travell cost:
Aye me, to see that gentle maide so tost!'
But Scudamour, then sighing deepe, thus saide:
'Certes her losse ought me to sorrow most,
Whose right she is, where ever she be straide,
Through many perils wonne, and many fortunes waide.

XXXIX
'For from the first that I her love profest,
Unto this houre, this present lucklesse howre,
I never joyed happinesse nor rest,
But thus turmoild from one to other stowre,
I wast my life, and doe my daies devowre
In wretched anguishe and incessant woe,
Passing the measure of my feeble powre,
That, living thus a wretch and loving so,
I neither can my love, ne yet my life forgo.'

XL
Then good Sir Claribell him thus bespake:
'Now were it not, Sir Scudamour, to you
Dislikefull paine, so sad a taske to take,
Mote we entreat you, sith this gentle crew
Is now so well accorded all anew,
That, as we ride together on our way,
Ye will recount to us in order dew
All that adventure, which ye did assay
For that faire ladies love: past perils well apay.'

XLI
So gan the rest him likewise to require,
But Britomart did him importune hard
To take on him that paine: whose great desire
He glad to satisfie, him selfe prepar'd
To tell through what misfortune he had far'd
In that atchievement, as to him befell;
And all those daungers unto them declar'd,
Which sith they cannot in this canto well
Comprised be, I will them in another tell.

CANTO X

Scudamour doth his conquest tell

Of vertuous Amoret:
Great Venus temple is describ'd,
And lovers life forth set.

I
'True he it said, what ever man it sayd,
That love with gall and hony doth abound,
But if the one be with the other wayd,
For every dram of hony therein found,
A pound of gall doth over it redound.
That I too true by triall have approved:
For since the day that first with deadly wound
My heart was launcht, and learned to have loved,
I never joyed howre, but still with care was moved.

II
'And yet such grace is given them from above,
That all the cares and evill which they meet
May nought at all their setled mindes remove,
But seeme, against common sence, to them most sweet;
As bosting in their martyrdome unmeet.
So all that ever yet I have endured
I count as naught, and tread downe under feet,
Since of my love at length I rest assured,
That to disloyalty she will not be allured.

III
'Long were to tell the travell and long toile,
Through which this Shield of Love I late have wonne,
And purchased this peerelesse beauties spoile,
That harder may be ended, then begonne:
But since ye so desire, your will be donne.
Then hearke, ye gentle knights and ladies free,
My hard mishaps, that ye may learne to shonne;
For though sweet love to conquer glorious bee,
Yet is the paine thereof much greater then the fee.

IV
'What time the fame of this renowmed prise
Flew first abroad, and all mens eares possest,
I, having armes then taken, gan avise
To winne me honour by some noble gest,
And purchase me some place amongst the best.
I boldly thought (so young mens thoughts are bold)
That this same brave emprize for me did rest,
And that both shield and she whom I behold
Might be my lucky lot; sith all by lot we hold.

V
'So on that hard adventure forth I went,

And to the place of perill shortly came.
That was a temple faire and auncient,
Which of great mother Venus bare the name,
And farre renowmed through exceeding fame;
Much more then that which was in Paphos built,
Or that in Cyprus, both long since this same,
Though all the pillours of the one were guilt,
And all the others pavement were with yvory spilt.

VI

'And it was seated in an island strong,
Abounding all with delices most rare,
And wall'd by nature gainst invaders wrong,
That none mote have accesse, nor inward fare,
But by one way, that passage did prepare.
It was a bridge ybuilt in goodly wize,
With curious corbes and pendants graven faire,
And, arched all with porches, did arize
On stately pillours, fram'd after the Doricke guize.

VII

'And for defence thereof, on th' other end
There reared was a castle faire and strong,
That warded all which in or out did wend,
And flancked both the bridges sides along,
Gainst all that would it faine to force or wrong.
And therein wonned twenty valiant knights;
All twenty tride in warres experience long;
Whose office was, against all manner wights
By all meanes to maintaine that castels ancient rights.

VIII

'Before that castle was an open plaine,
And in the midst thereof a piller placed;
On which this shield, of many sought in vaine,
The Shield of Love, whose guerdon me hath graced,
Was hangd on high with golden ribbands laced;
And in the marble stone was written this,
With golden letters goodly well enchaced:
Blessed the man that well can use his blis:
Whose ever be the shield, faire Amoret be his.

IX

'Which when I red, my heart did inly earne,
And pant with hope of that adventures hap:
Ne stayed further newes thereof to learne,
But with my speare upon the shield did rap,
That all the castle ringed with the clap.
Streight forth issewd a knight all arm'd to proofe,
And bravely mounted to his most mishap:
Who, staying nought to question from aloofe,

Ran fierce at me, that fire glaunst from his horses hoofe.

X
'Whom boldly I encountred as I could,
And by good fortune shortly him unseated.
Eftsoones out sprung two more of equall mould;
But I them both with equall hap defeated:
So all the twenty I likewise entreated,
And left them groning there upon the plaine.
Then, preacing to the pillour, I repeated
The read thereof for guerdon of my paine,
And taking downe the shield, with me did it retaine.

XI
'So forth without impediment I past,
Till to the bridges utter gate I came:
The which I found sure lockt and chained fast.
I knockt, but no man aunswred me by name;
I cald, but no man answerd to my clame.
Yet I persever'd still to knocke and call,
Till at the last I spide within the same
Where one stood peeping through a crevis small,
To whom I cald aloud, halfe angry therewithall.

XII
'That was to weet the porter of the place,
Unto whose trust the charge thereof was lent:
His name was Doubt, that had a double face,
Th' one forward looking, th' other backeward bent,
Therein resembling Janus aunceint,
Which hath in charge the ingate of the yeare:
And evermore his eyes about him went,
As if some proved perill he did feare,
Or did misdoubt some ill, whose cause did not appeare.

XIII
'On th' one side he, on th' other sate Delay,
Behinde the gate, that none her might espy;
Whose manner was, all passengers to stay
And entertaine with her occasions sly;
Through which some lost great hope unheedily,
Which never they recover might againe;
And others, quite excluded forth, did ly
Long languishing there in unpittied paine,
And seeking often entraunce afterwards in vaine.

XIV
'Me when as he had privily espide
Bearing the shield which I had conquerd late,
He kend it streight, and to me opened wide.
So in I past, and streight he closd the gate.

But being in, Delay in close awaite
Caught hold on me, and thought my steps to stay,
Feigning full many a fond excuse to prate,
And time to steale, the threasure of mans day,
Whose smallest minute lost no riches render may.

XV
'But by no meanes my way I would forslow,
For ought that ever she could doe or say,
But from my lofty steede dismounting low,
Past forth on foote, beholding all the way
The goodly workes, and stones of rich assay,
Cast into sundry shapes by wondrous skill,
That like on earth no where I recken may:
And underneath, the river rolling still
With murmure soft, that seem'd to serve the workmans will.

XVI
'Thence forth I passed to the second gate,
The Gate of Good Desert, whose goodly pride
And costly frame were long here to relate.
The same to all stoode alwaies open wide:
But in the porch did evermore abide
An hideous giant, dreadfull to behold,
That stopt the entraunce with his spacious stride,
And with the terrour of his countenance bold
Full many did affray, that else faine enter would.

XVII
'His name was Daunger, dreaded over all,
Who day and night did watch and duely ward,
From fearefull cowards entrance to forstall,
And faint-heart-fooles, whom shew of perill hard
Could terrifie from Fortunes faire adward:
For oftentimes faint hearts, at first espiall
Of his grim face, were from approaching scard:
Unworthy they of grace, whom one deniall
Excludes from fairest hope, withouten further triall.

XVIII
'Yet many doughty warriours, often tride
In greater perils to be stout and bold,
Durst not the sternnesse of his looke abide,
But soone as they his countenance did behold,
Began to faint, and feele their corage cold.
Againe, some other, that in hard assaies
Were cowards knowne, and litle count did hold,
Either through gifts, or guile, or such like waies,
Crept in by stouping low, or stealing of the kaies.

XIX

'But I, though meanest man of many moe,
Yet much disdaining unto him to lout,
Or creepe betweene his legs, so in to goe,
Resolv'd him to assault with manhood stout,
And either beat him in or drive him out.
Eftsoones, advauncing that enchaunted shield,
With all my might I gan to lay about:
Which when he saw, the glaive which he did wield
He gan forthwith t' avale, and way unto me yield.

XX
'So as I entred, I did backeward looke,
For feare of harme, that might lie hidden there;
And loe! his hindparts, whereof heed I tooke,
Much more deformed fearefull ugly were,
Then all his former parts did earst appere:
For Hatred, Murther, Treason, and Despight,
With many moe, lay in ambushment there,
Awayting to entrap the warelesse wight,
Which did not them prevent with vigilant foresight.

XXI
'Thus having past all perill, I was come
Within the compasse of that islands space;
The which did seeme, unto my simple doome,
The onely pleasant and delightfull place
That ever troden was of footings trace.
For all that Nature by her mother wit
Could frame in earth, and forme of substance base,
Was there, and all that Nature did omit,
Art, playing second Natures part, supplyed it.

XXII
'No tree, that is of count, in greenewood growes,
From lowest juniper to ceder tall,
No flowre in field, that daintie odour throwes,
And deckes his branch with blossomes over all,
But there was planted, or grew naturall:
Nor sense of man so coy and curious nice,
But there mote find to please it selfe withall;
Nor hart could wish for any queint device,
But there it present was, and did fraile sense entice.

XXIII
'In such luxurious plentie of all pleasure,
It seem'd a second paradise to ghesse,
So lavishly enricht with Natures threasure,
That if the happie soules, which doe possesse
Th' Elysian fields and live in lasting blesse,
Should happen this with living eye to see,
They soone would loath their lesser happinesse,

And wish to life return'd againe to bee,
That in this joyous place they mote have joyance free.

XXIV
'Fresh shadowes, fit to shroud from sunny ray;
Faire lawnds, to take the sunne in season dew;
Sweet springs, in which a thousand nymphs did play;
Soft rombling brookes, that gentle slomber drew;
High reared mounts, the lands about to vew;
Low looking dales, disloignd from common gaze;
Delightfull bowres, to solace lovers trew;
False labyrinthes, fond runners eyes to daze;
All which by Nature made did Nature selfe amaze.

XXV
'And all without were walkes and alleyes dight
With divers trees, enrang'd in even rankes;
And here and there were pleasant arbors pight,
And shadie seates, and sundry flowring bankes,
To sit and rest the walkers wearie shankes;
And therein thousand payres of lovers walkt,
Praysing their god, and yeelding him great thankes,
Ne ever ought but of their true loves talkt,
Ne ever for rebuke or blame of any balkt.

XXVI
'All these together by themselves did sport
Their spotlesse pleasures, and sweet loves content.
But farre away from these, another sort
Of lovers lincked in true harts consent;
Which loved not as these, for like intent,
But on chast vertue grounded their desire,
Farre from all fraud, or fayned blandishment;
Which, in their spirits kindling zealous fire,
Brave thoughts and noble deedes did evermore aspire.

XXVII
'Such were great Hercules, and Hyllus deare;
Trew Jonathan, and David trustie tryde;
Stout Theseus, and Pirithous his feare;
Pylades, and Orestes by his syde;
Myld Titus and Gesippus without pryde;
Damon and Pythias, whom death could not sever:
All these, and all that ever had bene tyde
In bands of friendship, there did live for ever;
Whose lives although decay'd, yet loves decayed never.

XXVIII
'Which when as I, that never tasted blis
Nor happie howre, beheld with gazefull eye,
I thought there was none other heaven then this;

And gan their endlesse happinesse envye,
That, being free from feare and gealosye,
Might frankely there their loves desire possesse;
Whilest I through paines and perlous jeopardie
Was forst to seeke my lifes deare patronesse:
Much dearer be the things which come through hard distresse.

XXIX
'Yet all those sights, and all that else I saw,
Might not my steps withhold, but that forthright
Unto that purposd place I did me draw,
Where as my love was lodged day and night:
The temple of great Venus, that is hight
The Queene of Beautie, and of Love the mother,
There worshipped of every living wight;
Whose goodly workmanship farre past all other
That ever were on earth, all were they set together.

XXX
'Not that same famous temple of Diane,
Whose hight all Ephesus did oversee,
And which all Asia sought with vowes prophane,
One of the worlds seven wonders sayd to bee,
Might match with this by many a degree:
Nor that which that wise king of Jurie framed,
With endlesse cost, to be th' Almighties see;
Nor all that else through all the world is named
To all the heathen gods, might like to this be clamed.

XXXI
'I, much admyring that so goodly frame,
Unto the porch approcht, which open stood;
But therein sate an amiable dame,
That seem'd to be of very sober mood,
And in her semblant shewed great womanhood:
Strange was her tyre; for on her head a crowne
She wore, much like unto a Danisk hood,
Poudred with pearle and stone, and all her gowne
Enwoven was with gold, that raught full low a downe.

XXXII
'On either side of her two young men stood,
Both strongly arm'd, as fearing one another;
Yet were they brethren both of halfe the blood,
Begotten by two fathers of one mother,
Though of contrarie natures each to other:
The one of them hight Love, the other Hate;
Hate was the elder, Love the younger brother;
Yet was the younger stronger in his state
Then th' elder, and him maystred still in all debate.

XXXIII
'Nathlesse that dame so well them tempred both,
That she them forced hand to joyne in hand,
Albe that Hatred was thereto full loth,
And turn'd his face away, as he did stand,
Unwilling to behold that lovely band.
Yet she was of such grace and vertuous might,
That her commaundment he could not withstand,
But bit his lip for felonous despight,
And gnasht his yron tuskes at that displeasing sight.

XXXIV
'Concord she cleeped was in common reed,
Mother of blessed Peace and Friendship trew;
They both her twins, both borne of heavenly seed,
And she her selfe likewise divinely grew;
The which right well her workes divine did shew:
For strength and wealth and happinesse she lends,
And strife and warre and anger does subdew;
Of litle much, of foes she maketh frends,
And to afflicted minds sweet rest and quiet sends.

XXXV
'By her the heaven is in his course contained,
And all the world in state unmoved stands,
As their Almightie Maker first ordained,
And bound them with inviolable bands;
Else would the waters overflow the lands,
And fire devoure the ayre, and hell them quight,
But that she holds them with her blessed hands.
She is the nourse of pleasure and delight,
And unto Venus grace the gate doth open right.

XXXVI
'By her I entring halfe dismayed was,
But she in gentle wise me entertayned,
And twixt her selfe and Love did let me pas;
But Hatred would my entrance have restrayned,
And with his club me threatned to have brayned,
Had not the ladie with her powrefull speach
Him from his wicked will uneath refrayned;
And th' other eke his malice did empeach,
Till I was throughly past the perill of his reach.

XXXVII
'Into the inmost temple thus I came,
Which fuming all with frankensence I found,
And odours rising from the altars flame.
Upon an hundred marble pillors round
The roofe up high was reared from the ground,
All deckt with crownes, and chaynes, and girlands gay,

And thousand pretious gifts worth many a pound,
The which sad lovers for their vowes did pay;
And all the ground was strow'd with flowres, as fresh as May.

XXXVIII
'An hundred altars round about were set,
All flaming with their sacrifices fire,
That with the steme thereof the temple swet,
Which rould in clouds to heaven did aspire,
And in them bore true lovers vowes entire:
And eke an hundred brasen caudrons bright,
To bath in joy and amorous desire,
Every of which was to a damzell hight;
For all the priests were damzels, in soft linnen dight.

XXXIX
'Right in the midst the goddesse selfe did stand
Upon an altar of some costly masse,
Whose substance was uneath to understand:
For neither pretious stone, nor durefull brasse,
Nor shining gold, nor mouldring clay it was;
But much more rare and pretious to esteeme,
Pure in aspect, and like to christall glasse,
Yet glasse was not, if one did rightly deeme,
But being faire and brickle, likest glasse did seeme.

XL
'But it in shape and beautie did excell
All other idoles which the heathen adore,
Farre passing that which by surpassing skill
Phidias did make in Paphos isle of yore,
With which that wretched Greeke, that life forlore,
Did fall in love: yet this much fairer shined,
But covered with a slender veile afore;
And both her feete and legs together twyned
Were with a snake, whose head and tail were fast combyned.

XLI
'The cause why she was covered with a vele
Was hard to know, for that her priests the same
From peoples knowledge labour'd to concele.
But sooth it was not sure for womanish shame,
Nor any blemish, which the worke mote blame;
But for, they say, she hath both kinds in one,
Both male and female, both under one name:
She syre and mother is her selfe alone,
Begets and eke conceives, ne needeth other none.

XLII
'And all about her necke and shoulders flew
A flocke of litle loves, and sports, and joyes,

With nimble wings of gold and purple hew,
Whose shapes seem'd not like to terrestriall boyes,
But like to angels playing heavenly toyes;
The whilest their eldest brother was away,
Cupid, their eldest brother: he enjoyes
The wide kingdome of Love with lordly sway,
And to his law compels all creatures to obay.

XLIII
'And all about her altar, scattered lay
Great sorts of lovers piteously complayning,
Some of their losse, some of their loves delay,
Some of their pride, some paragons disdayning,
Some fearing fraud, some fraudulently fayning,
As every one had cause of good or ill.
Amongst the rest some one, through loves constrayning,
Tormented sore, could not containe it still,
But thus brake forth, that all the temple it did fill:

XLIV
'"Great Venus, queene of beautie and of grace,
The joy of gods and men, that under skie
Doest fayrest shine, and most adorne thy place,
That with thy smyling looke doest pacifie
The raging seas, and makst the stormes to flie;
Thee, goddesse, thee the winds, the clouds doe feare,
And when thou spredst thy mantle forth on hie,
The waters play, and pleasant lands appeare,
And heavens laugh, and al the world shews joyous cheare.

XLV
'"Then doth the dædale earth throw forth to thee
Out of her fruitfull lap aboundant flowres;
And then all living wights, soone as they see
The Spring breake forth out of his lusty bowres,
They all doe learne to play the paramours:
First doe the merry birds, thy prety pages,
Privily pricked with thy lustfull powres,
Chirpe loud to thee out of their leavy cages,
And thee their mother call to coole their kindly rages.

XLVI
'"Then doe the salvage beasts begin to play
Their pleasant friskes, and loath their wonted food;
The lyons rore, the tygres loudly bray,
The raging buls rebellow through the wood,
And breaking forth, dare tempt the deepest flood,
To come where thou doest draw them with desire:
So all things else, that nourish vitall blood,
Soone as with fury thou doest them inspire,
In generation seeke to quench their inward fire.

XLVII
'"So all the world by thee at first was made,
And dayly yet thou doest the same repayre:
Ne ought on earth that merry is and glad,
Ne ought on earth that lovely is and fayre,
But thou the same for pleasure didst prepayre.
Thou art the root of all that joyous is,
Great god of men and women, queene of th' ayre,
Mother of laughter, and welspring of blisse;
O graunt that of my love at last I may not misse."

XLVIII
'So did he say: but I with murmure soft,
That none might heare the sorrow of my hart,
Yet inly groning deepe and sighing oft,
Besought her to graunt ease unto my smart,
And to my wound her gratious help impart.
Whilest thus I spake, behold! with happy eye
I spyde where at the idoles feet apart
A bevie of fayre damzels close did lye,
Wayting when as the antheme should be sung on hye.

XLIX
'The first of them did seeme of ryper yeares
And graver countenance then all the rest;
Yet all the rest were eke her equall peares,
Yet unto her obayed all the best.
Her name was Womanhood, that she exprest
By her sad semblant and demeanure wyse:
For stedfast still her eyes did fixed rest,
Ne rov'd at randon, after gazers guyse,
Whose luring baytes oftimes doe heedlesse harts entyse.

L
'And next to her sate goodly Shamefastnesse,
Ne ever durst her eyes from ground upreare,
Ne ever once did looke up from her desse,
As if some blame of evill she did feare,
That in her cheekes made roses oft appeare:
And her against sweet Cherefulnesse was placed,
Whose eyes, like twinkling stars in evening cleare,
Were deckt with smyles, that all sad humors chaced,
And darted forth delights, the which her goodly graced.

LI
'And next to her sate sober Modestie,
Holding her hand upon her gentle hart;
And her against sate comely Curtesie,
That unto every person knew her part;
And her before was seated overthwart

Soft Silence, and submisse Obedience,
Both linckt together never to dispart,
Both gifts of God not gotten but from thence,
Both girlonds of his saints against their foes offence.

LII
'Thus sate they all a round in seemely rate.
And in the midst of them a goodly mayd,
Even in the lap of Womanhood, there sate,
The which was all in lilly white arayd,
With silver streames amongst the linnen stray'd;
Like to the Morne, when first her shyning face
Hath to the gloomy world it selfe bewray'd:
That same was fayrest Amoret in place,
Shyning with beauties light and heavenly vertues grace.

LIII
'Whom soone as I beheld, my hart gan throb,
And wade in doubt, what best were to be donne:
For sacrilege me seem'd the church to rob,
And folly seem'd to leave the thing undonne,
Which with so strong attempt I had begonne.
Tho, shaking off all doubt and shamefast feare,
Which ladies love I heard had never wonne
Mongst men of worth, I to her stepped neare,
And by the lilly hand her labour'd up to reare.

LIV
'Thereat that formost matrone me did blame,
And sharpe rebuke, for being over bold;
Saying it was to knight unseemely shame,
Upon a recluse virgin to lay hold,
That unto Venus services was sold.
To whom I thus: "Nay, but it fitteth best
For Cupids man with Venus mayd to hold;
For ill your goddesse services are drest
By virgins, and her sacrifices let to rest."

LV
'With that my shield I forth to her did show,
Which all that while I closely had conceld;
On which when Cupid with his killing bow
And cruell shafts emblazond she beheld,
At sight thereof she was with terror queld,
And said no more: but I, which all that while
The pledge of faith, her hand, engaged held,
Like warie hynd within the weedie soyle,
For no intreatie would forgoe so glorious spoyle.

LVI
'And evermore upon the goddesse face

Mine eye was fixt, for feare of her offence:
Whom when I saw with amiable grace
To laugh at me, and favour my pretence,
I was emboldned with more confidence,
And nought for nicenesse nor for envy sparing,
In presence of them all forth led her thence,
All looking on, and like astonisht staring,
Yet to lay hand on her not one of all them daring.

LVII
'She often prayd, and often me besought,
Sometime with tender teares to let her goe,
Sometime with witching smyles: but yet, for nought
That ever she to me could say or doe,
Could she her wished freedome fro me wooe;
But forth I led her through the temple gate,
By which I hardly past with much adoe:
But that same ladie, which me friended late
In entrance, did me also friend in my retrate.

LVIII
'No lesse did Daunger threaten me with dread,
When as he saw me, maugre all his powre,
That glorious spoyle of beautie with me lead,
Then Cerberus, when Orpheus did recoure
His leman from the Stygian princes boure.
But evermore my shield did me defend
Against the storme of every dreadfull stoure:
Thus safely with my love I thence did wend.'
So ended he his tale, where I this canto end.

CANTO XI

Marinells former wound is heald;
He comes to Proteus hall,
Where Thames doth the Medway wedd,
And feasts the sea-gods all.

I
But ah for pittie that I have thus long
Left a fayre ladie languishing in payne!
Now well away! that I have doen such wrong,
To let faire Florimell in bands remayne,
In bands of love, and in sad thraldomes chayne!
From which unlesse some heavenly powre her free
By miracle, not yet appearing playne,
She lenger yet is like captiv'd to bee:

That even to thinke thereof it inly pitties mee.

II
Here neede you to remember, how erewhile
Unlovely Proteus, missing to his mind
That virgins love to win by wit or wile,
Her threw into a dongeon deepe and blind,
And there in chaynes her cruelly did bind,
In hope thereby her to his bent to draw:
For when as neither gifts nor graces kind
Her constant mind could move at all, he saw,
He thought her to compell by crueltie and awe.

III
Deepe in the bottome of an huge great rocke
The dongeon was, in which her bound he left,
That neither yron barres, nor brasen locke,
Did neede to gard from force or secret theft
Of all her lovers, which would her have reft.
For wall'd it was with waves, which rag'd and ror'd
As they the cliffe in peeces would have cleft;
Besides, ten thousand monsters foule abhor'd
Did waite about it, gaping griesly, all begor'd.

IV
And in the midst thereof did horror dwell,
And darkenesse dredd, that never viewed day,
Like to the balefull house of lowest hell,
In which old Styx her aged bones alway,
Old Styx the grandame of the gods, doth lay.
There did this lucklesse mayd seven months abide,
Ne ever evening saw, ne mornings ray,
Ne ever from the day the night descride,
But thought it all one night, that did no houres divide.

V
And all this was for love of Marinell,
Who her despysd (ah! who would her despyse?)
And wemens love did from his hart expell,
And all those joyes that weake mankind entyse.
Nathlesse his pride full dearely he did pryse;
For of a womans hand it was ywroke,
That of the wound he yet in languor lyes,
Ne can be cured of that cruell stroke
Which Britomart him gave, when he did her provoke.

VI
Yet farre and neare the nymph, his mother, sought,
And many salves did to his sore applie,
And many herbes did use. But when as nought
She saw could ease his rankling maladie,

At last to Tryphon she for helpe did hie,
(This Tryphon is the seagods surgeon hight)
Whom she besought to find some remedie:
And for his paines a whistle him behight,
That of a fishes shell was wrought with rare delight.

VII
So well that leach did hearke to her request,
And did so well employ his carefull paine,
That in short space his hurts he had redrest,
And him restor'd to healthfull state againe:
In which he long time after did remaine
There with the nymph his mother, like her thrall;
Who sore against his will did him retaine,
For feare of perill, which to him mote fall,
Through his too ventrous prowesse proved over all.

VIII
It fortun'd then, a solemne feast was there
To all the sea-gods and their fruitfull seede,
In honour of the spousalls which then were
Betwixt the Medway and the Thames agreed.
Long had the Thames (as we in records reed)
Before that day her wooed to his bed;
But the proud nymph would for no worldly meed,
Nor no entreatie to his love be led;
Till now at last relenting, she to him was wed.

IX
So both agreed that this their bridale feast
Should for the gods in Proteus house be made;
To which they all repayr'd, both most and least,
Aswell which in the mightie ocean trade,
As that in rivers swim, or brookes doe wade.
All which not if an hundred tongues to tell,
And hundred mouthes, and voice of brasse I had,
And endlesse memorie, that mote excell,
In order as they came, could I recount them well.

X
Helpe therefore, O thou sacred imp of Jove,
The noursling of Dame Memorie his deare,
To whom those rolles, layd up in heaven above,
And records of antiquitie appeare,
To which no wit of man may comen neare;
Helpe me to tell the names of all those floods,
And all those nymphes, which then assembled were
To that great banquet of the watry gods,
And all their sundry kinds, and all their hid abodes.

XI

First came great Neptune with his three-forkt mace,
That rules the seas, and makes them rise or fall;
His dewy lockes did drop with brine apace,
Under his diademe imperiall:
And by his side his queene with coronall,
Faire Amphitrite, most divinely faire,
Whose yvorie shoulders weren covered all,
As with a robe, with her owne silver haire,
And deckt with pearles, which th' Indian seas for her prepaire.

XII
These marched farre afore the other crew;
And all the way before them as they went,
Triton his trompet shrill before them blew,
For goodly triumph and great jollyment,
That made the rockes to roare, as they were rent.
And after them the royall issue came,
Which of them sprung by lineall descent:
First the sea-gods, which to themselves doe clame
The powre to rule the billowes, and the waves to tame:

XIII
Phorcys, the father of that fatall brood,
By whom those old heroes wonne such fame;
And Glaucus, that wise southsayes understood;
And tragicke Inoes sonne, the which became
A god of seas through his mad mothers blame,
Now hight Palemon, and is saylers frend;
Great Brontes, and Astræus, that did shame
Himselfe with incest of his kin unkend;
And huge Orion, that doth tempests still portend;

XIV
The rich Cteatus, and Eurytus long;
Neleus and Pelias, lovely brethren both;
Mightie Chrysaor, and Caïcus strong;
Eurypulus, that calmes the waters wroth;
And faire Euphœmus, that upon them goth
As on the ground, without dismay or dread;
Fierce Eryx, and Alebius that know'th
The waters depth, and doth their bottome tread;
And sad Asopus, comely with his hoarie head.

XV
There also some most famous founders were
Of puissant nations, which the world possest;
Yet sonnes of Neptune, now assembled here:
Ancient Ogyges, even th' auncientest,
And Inachus renowmd above the rest;
Phœnix, and Aon, and Pelasgus old,
Great Belus, Phœax, and Agenor best;

And mightie Albion, father of the bold
And warlike people which the Britaine Islands hold.

XVI
For Albion the sonne of Neptune was,
Who, for the proofe of his great puissance,
Out of his Albion did on dry-foot pas
Into old Gall, that now is cleeped France,
To fight with Hercules, that did advance
To vanquish all the world with matchlesse might,
And there his mortall part by great mischance
Was slaine: but that which is th' immortall spright
Lives still, and to this feast with Neptunes seed was dight.

XVII
But what doe I their names seeke to reherse,
Which all the world have with their issue fild?
How can they all in this so narrow verse
Contayned be, and in small compasse hild?
Let them record them, that are better skild,
And know the moniments of passed age:
Onely what needeth shall be here fulfild,
T' expresse some part of that great equipage,
Which from great Neptune do derive their parentage.

XVIII
Next came the aged Ocean, and his dame,
Old Tethys, th' oldest two of all the rest,
For all the rest of those two parents came,
Which afterward both sea and land possest:
Of all which Nereus, th' eldest and the best,
Did first proceed, then which none more upright,
Ne more sincere in word and deed profest;
Most voide of guile, most free from fowle despight,
Doing him selfe, and teaching others to doe right.

XIX
Thereto he was expert in prophecies,
And could the ledden of the gods unfold,
Through which, when Paris brought his famous prise,
The faire Tindarid lasse, he him fortold,
That her all Greece with many a champion bold
Should fetch againe, and finally destroy
Proud Priams towne. So wise is Nereus old,
And so well skild; nathlesse he takes great joy
Oft-times amongst the wanton nymphs to sport and toy.

XX
And after him the famous rivers came,
Which doe the earth enrich and beautifie:
The fertile Nile, which creatures new doth frame;

Long Rhodanus, whose sourse springs from the skie;
Faire Ister, flowing from the mountaines hie;
Divine Scamander, purpled yet with blood
Of Greekes and Trojans, which therein did die;
Pactolus glistring with his golden flood,
And Tygris fierce, whose streames of none may be withstood;

XXI
Great Ganges, and immortall Euphrates,
Deepe Indus, and Mæander intricate,
Slow Peneus, and tempestuous Phasides,
Swift Rhene, and Alpheus still immaculate;
Ooraxes, feared for great Cyrus fate;
Tybris, renowmed for the Romaines fame;
Rich Oranochy, though but knowen late;
And that huge river, which doth beare his name
Of warlike Amazons, which doe possesse the same.

XXII
Joy on those warlike women, which so long
Can from all men so rich a kingdome hold!
And shame on you, O men, which boast your strong
And valiant hearts, in thoughts lesse hard and bold,
Yet quaile in conquest of that land of gold!
But this to you, O Britons, most pertaines,
To whom the right hereof it selfe hath sold;
The which, for sparing litle cost or paines,
Loose so immortall glory, and so endlesse gaines.

XXIII
Then was there heard a most celestiall sound
Of dainty musicke, which did next ensew
Before the spouse: that was Arion crownd;
Who, playing on his harpe, unto him drew
The eares and hearts of all that goodly crew,
That even yet the dolphin, which him bore
Through the Agæan seas from pirates vew,
Stood still by him astonisht at his lore,
And all the raging seas for joy forgot to rore.

XXIV
So went he playing on the watery plaine.
Soone after whom the lovely bridegroome came,
The noble Thamis, with all his goodly traine;
But him before there went, as best became,
His auncient parents, namely th' aunclent Thame:
But much more aged was his wife then he,
The Ouze, whom men doe Isis rightly name;
Full weake and crooked creature seemed shee,
And almost blind through eld, that scarce her way could see.

XXV
Therefore on either side she was sustained
Of two smal grooms, which by their names were hight
The Churne and Charwell, two small streames, which pained
Them selves her footing to direct aright,
Which fayled oft through faint and feeble plight:
But Thame was stronger, and of better stay;
Yet seem'd full aged by his outward sight,
With head all hoary, and his beard all gray,
Deawed with silver drops, that trickled downe alway.

XXVI
And eke he somewhat seem'd to stoupe afore
With bowed backe, by reason of the lode
And aunciect heavy burden which he bore
Of that faire city, wherein make abode
So many learned impes, that shoote abrode,
And with their braunches spred all Britany,
No lesse then do her elder sisters broode.
Joy to you both, ye double noursery
Of arts! but, Oxford, thine doth Thame most glorify.

XXVII
But he their sonne full fresh and jolly was,
All decked in a robe of watchet hew,
On which the waves, glittering like christall glas,
So cunningly enwoven were, that few
Could weenen whether they were false or trew.
And on his head like to a coronet
He wore, that seemed strange to common vew,
In which were many towres and castels set,
That it encompast round as with a golden fret.

XXVIII
Like as the mother of the gods, they say,
In her great iron charet wonts to ride,
When to Joves pallace she doth take her way,
Old Cybele, arayd with pompous pride,
Wearing a diademe embattild wide
With hundred turrets, like a turribant.
With such an one was Thamis beautifide;
That was to weet the famous Troynovant,
In which her kingdomes throne is chiefly resiant.

XXIX
And round about him many a pretty page
Attended duely, ready to obay;
All little rivers, which owe vassallage
To him, as to their lord, and tribute pay:
The chaulky Kenet, and the Thetis gray,
The morish Cole, and the soft sliding Breane,

The wanton Lee, that oft doth loose his way,
And the still Darent, in whose waters cleane
Ten thousand fishes play, and decke his pleasant streame.

XXX
Then came his neighbour flouds, which nigh him dwell,
And water all the English soile throughout;
They all on him this day attended well,
And with meet service waited him about;
Ne none disdained low to him to lout:
No, not the stately Severne grudg'd at all,
Ne storming Humber, though he looked stout;
But both him honor'd as their principall,
And let their swelling waters low before him fall.

XXXI
There was the speedy Tamar, which devides
The Cornish and the Devonish confines;
Through both whose borders swiftly downe it glides,
And meeting Plim, to Plimmouth thence declines:
And Dart, nigh chockt with sands of tinny mines.
But Avon marched in more stately path,
Proud of his adamants, with which he shines
And glisters wide, as als' of wondrous Bath,
And Bristow faire, which on his waves he builded hath.

XXXII
And there came Stoure with terrible aspect,
Bearing his sixe deformed heads on hye,
That doth his course through Blandford plains direct,
And washeth Winborne meades in season drye.
Next him went Wylibourne with passage slye,
That of his wylinesse his name doth take,
And of him selfe doth name the shire thereby:
And Mole, that like a nousling mole doth make
His way still under ground, till Thamis he overtake.

XXXIII
Then came the Rother, decked all with woods
Like a wood god, and flowing fast to Rhy:
And Sture, that parteth with his pleasant floods
The easterne Saxons from the southerne ny,
And Clare and Harwitch both doth beautify:
Him follow'd Yar, soft washing Norwitch wall,
And with him brought a present joyfully
Of his owne fish unto their festivall,
Whose like none else could shew, the which they ruffins call.

XXXIV
Next these the plenteous Ouse came far from land,
By many a city, and by many a towne,

And many rivers taking under hand
Into his waters, as he passeth downe,
The Cle, the Were, the Grant, the Sture, the Rowne,
Thence doth by Huntingdon and Cambridge flit,
My mother Cambridge, whom as with a crowne
He doth adorne, and is adorn'd of it
With many a gentle muse, and many a learned wit.

XXXV
And after him the fatall Welland went,
That if old sawes prove true (which God forbid)
Shall drowne all Holland with his excrement,
And shall see Stamford, though now homely hid,
Then shine in learning, more then ever did
Cambridge or Oxford, Englands goodly beames.
And next to him the Nene downe softly slid;
And bounteous Trent, that in him selfe enseames
Both thirty sorts of fish and thirty sundry streames.

XXXVI
Next these came Tyne, along whose stony bancke
That Romaine monarch built a brasen wall,
Which mote the feebled Britons strongly flancke
Against the Picts, that swarmed over all,
Which yet thereof Gualsever they doe call:
And Twede, the limit betwixt Logris land
And Albany: and Eden, though but small,
Yet often stainde with bloud of many a band
Of Scots and English both, that tyned on his strand.

XXXVII
Then came those sixe sad brethren, like forlorne,
That whilome were (as antique fathers tell)
Sixe valiant knights, of one faire nymphe yborne,
Which did in noble deedes of armes excell,
And wonned there where now Yorke people dwell:
Still Ure, swift Werfe, and Oze the most of might,
High Swale, unquiet Nide, and troublous Skell;
All whom a Scythian king, that Humber hight,
Slew cruelly, and in the river drowned quight.

XXXVIII
But past not long, ere Brutus warlicke sonne,
Locrinus, them aveng'd, and the same date,
Which the proud Humber unto them had donne,
By equall dome repayd on his owne pate:
For in the selfe same river, where he late
Had drenched them, he drowned him againe;
And nam'd the river of his wretched fate;
Whose bad condition yet it doth retaine,
Oft tossed with his stormes, which therein still remaine.

XXXIX
These after, came the stony shallow Lone,
That to old Loncaster his name doth lend;
And following Dee, which Britons long ygone
Did call divine, that doth by Chester tend;
And Conway, which out of his streame doth send
Plenty of pearles to decke his dames withall;
And Lindus, that his pikes doth most commend,
Of which the auncient Lincolne men doe call:
All these together marched toward Proteus hall.

XL
Ne thence the Irishe rivers absent were:
Sith no lesse famous then the rest they bee,
And joyne in neighbourhood of kingdome nere,
Why should they not likewise in love agree,
And joy likewise this solemne day to see?
They saw it all, and present were in place;
Though I them all, according their degree,
Cannot recount, nor tell their hidden race,
Nor read the salvage cuntreis thorough which they pace.

XLI
There was the Liffy rolling downe the lea,
The sandy Slane, the stony Aubrian,
The spacious Shenan spreading like a sea,
The pleasant Boyne, the fishy fruitfull Ban,
Swift Awniduff, which of the English man
Is cal'de Blackewater, and the Liffar deep,
Sad Trowis, that once his people overran,
Strong Allo tombling from Slewlogher steep,
And Mulla mine, whose waves I whilom taught to weep.

XLII
And there the three renowmed brethren were,
Which that great gyant Blomius begot
Of the faire nimph Rheusa wandring there.
One day, as she to shunne the season whot,
Under Slewbloome in shady grove was got,
This gyant found her, and by force deflowr'd;
Whereof conceiving, she in time forth brought
These three faire sons, which, being thence forth powrd,
In three great rivers ran, and many countreis scowrd.

XLIII
The first, the gentle Shure, that, making way
By sweet Clonmell, adornes rich Waterford;
The next, the stubborne Newre, whose waters gray
By faire Kilkenny and Rosseponte boord;
The third, the goodly Barow, which doth hoord

Great heapes of salmons in his deepe bosome:
All which long sundred, doe at last accord
To joyne in one, ere to the sea they come,
So, flowing all from one, all one at last become.

XLIV
There also was the wide embayed Mayre,
The pleasaunt Bandon, crownd with many a wood,
The spreading Lee, that like an island fayre
Encloseth Corke with his devided flood;
And balefull Oure, late staind with English blood:
With many more, whose names no tongue can tell.
All which that day in order seemly good
Did on the Thamis attend, and waited well
To doe their duefull service, as to them befell.

XLV
Then came the bride, the lovely Medua came,
Clad in a vesture of unknowen geare,
And uncouth fashion, yet her well became;
That seem'd like silver, sprinckled here and theare
With glittering spangs, that did like starres appeare,
And wav'd upon, like water chamelot,
To hide the metall, which yet every where
Bewrayd it selfe, to let men plainely wot,
It was no mortall worke, that seem'd and yet was not.

XLVI
Her goodly lockes adowne her backe did flow
Unto her waste, with flowres bescattered,
The which ambrosiall odours forth did throw
To all about, and all her shoulders spred
As a new spring; and likewise on her hed
A chapelet of sundry flowers she wore,
From under which the deawy humour shed
Did tricle downe her haire, like to the hore
Congealed litle drops, which doe the morne adore.

XLVII
On her two pretty handmaides did attend,
One cald the Theise, the other cald the Crane;
Which on her waited, things amisse to mend,
And both behind upheld her spredding traine;
Under the which her feet appeared plaine,
Her silver feet, faire washt against this day:
And her before there paced pages twaine,
Both clad in colours like, and like array,
The Doune and eke the Frith, both which prepard her way.

XLVIII
And after these the sea nymphs marched all,

All goodly damzels, deckt with long greene haire,
Whom of their sire Nereides men call,
All which the Oceans daughter to him bare,
The gray eyde Doris: all which fifty are;
All which she there on her attending had:
Swift Proto, milde Eucrate, Thetis faire,
Soft Spio, sweete Eudore, Sao sad,
Light Doto, wanton Glauce, and Galene glad,

XLIX
White hand Eunica, proud Dynamene,
Joyous Thalia, goodly Amphitrite,
Lovely Pasithee, kinde Eulimene,
Light foote Cymothoe, and sweete Melite,
Fairest Pherusa, Phao lilly white,
Wondred Agave, Poris, and Nesæa,
With Erato, that doth in love delite,
And Panopæ, and wise Protomedæa,
And snowy neckd Doris, and milkewhite Galathæa,

L
Speedy Hippothoe, and chaste Actea,
Large Lisianassa, and Pronæa sage,
Evagore, and light Pontoporea,
And she that with her least word can asswage
The surging seas, when they do sorest rage,
Cymodoce, and stout Autonoe,
And Neso, and Eione well in age,
And seeming still to smile, Glauconome,
And she that hight of many heastes Polynome,

LI
Fresh Alimeda, deckt with girlond greene,
Hyponeo, with salt bedewed wrests,
Laomedia, like the christall sheene,
Liagore, much praisd for wise behests,
And Psamathe, for her brode snowy brests,
Cymo, Eupompe, and Themiste just,
And she that vertue loves and vice detests,
Evarna, and Menippe true in trust,
And Nemertea, learned well to rule her lust.

LII
All these the daughters of old Nereus were,
Which have the sea in charge to them assinde,
To rule his tides, and surges to uprere,
To bring forth stormes, or fast them to upbinde,
And sailers save from wreckes of wrathfull winde.
And yet besides, three thousand more there were
Of th' Oceans seede, but Joves and Phœbus kinde;
The which in floods and fountaines doe appere,

And all mankinde do nourish with their waters clere.

LIII
The which, more eath it were for mortall wight
To tell the sands, or count the starres on hye,
Or ought more hard, then thinke to reckon right.
But well I wote that these which I descry
Were present at this great solemnity:
And there, amongst the rest, the mother was
Of luckelesse Marinell, Cymodoce;
Which, for my Muse her selfe now tyred has,
Unto an other canto I will overpas.

CANTO XII

Marin, for love of Florimell,
In languor wastes his life:
The nymph his mother getteth her,
And gives to him for wife.

I
O what an endlesse worke have I in hand,
To count the seas abundant progeny,
Whose fruitfull seede farre passeth those in land,
And also those which wonne in th' azure sky!
For much more eath to tell the starres on hy,
Albe they endlesse seeme in estimation,
Then to recount the seas posterity:
So fertile be the flouds in generation,
So huge their numbers, and so numberlesse their nation.

II
Therefore the antique wisards well invented,
That Venus of the fomy sea was bred;
For that the seas by her are most augmented.
Witnesse th' exceeding fry which there are fed,
And wondrous sholes, which may of none be red.
Then blame me not, if I have err'd in count
Of gods, of nymphs, of rivers yet unred:
For though their numbers do much more surmount,
Yet all those same were there, which erst I did recount.

III
All those were there, and many other more,
Whose names and nations were too long to tell,
That Proteus house they fild even to the dore;
Yet were they all in order, as befell,

According their degrees disposed well.
Amongst the rest was faire Cymodoce,
The mother of unlucky Marinell,
Who thither with her came, to learne and see
The manner of the gods when they at banquet be.

IV
But for he was halfe mortall, being bred
Of mortall sire, though of immortall wombe,
He might not with immortall food be fed,
Ne with th' eternall gods to bancket come;
But walkt abrode, and round about did rome,
To view the building of that uncouth place,
That seem'd unlike unto his earthly home:
Where, as he to and fro by chaunce did trace,
There unto him betid a disaventrous case.

V
Under the hanging of an hideous clieffe
He heard the lamentable voice of one
That piteously complaind her carefull grieffe,
Which never she before disclosd to none,
But to her selfe her sorrow did bemone.
So feelingly her case she did complaine,
That ruth it moved in the rocky stone,
And made it seeme to feele her grievous paine,
And oft to grone with billowes beating from the maine.

VI
'Though vaine I see my sorrowes to unfold,
And count my cares, when none is nigh to heare,
Yet, hoping griefe may lessen being told,
I will them tell though unto no man neare:
For Heaven, that unto all lends equall eare,
Is farre from hearing of my heavy plight;
And lowest Hell, to which I lie most neare,
Cares not what evils hap to wretched wight;
And greedy seas doe in the spoile of life delight.

VII
'Yet loe! the seas I see by often beating
Doe pearce the rockes, and hardest marble weares;
But his hard rocky hart for no entreating
Will yeeld, but when my piteous plaints he heares,
Is hardned more with my aboundant teares.
Yet though he never list to me relent,
But let me waste in woe my wretched yeares,
Yet will I never of my love repent,
But joy that for his sake I suffer prisonment.

VIII

'And when my weary ghost, with griefe outworne,
By timely death shall winne her wished rest,
Let then this plaint unto his eares be borne,
That blame it is to him, that armes profest,
To let her die, whom he might have redrest.'
There did she pause, inforced to give place
Unto the passion that her heart opprest;
And after she had wept and wail'd a space,
She gan afresh thus to renew her wretched case:

IX
'Ye gods of seas, if any gods at all
Have care of right, or ruth of wretches wrong,
By one or other way me, woefull thrall,
Deliver hence out of this dungeon strong,
In which I daily dying am too long.
And if ye deeme me death for loving one
That loves not me, then doe it not prolong,
But let me die and end my daies attone,
And let him live unlov'd, or love him selfe alone.

X
'But if that life ye unto me decree,
Then let mee live as lovers ought to do,
And of my lifes deare love beloved be:
And if he shall through pride your doome undo,
Do you by duresse him compell thereto,
And in this prison put him here with me:
One prison fittest is to hold us two:
So had I rather to be thrall then free;
Such thraldome or such freedome let it surely be.

XI
'But O vaine judgement, and conditions vaine,
The which the prisoner points unto the free!
The whiles I him condemne, and deeme his paine,
He where he list goes loose, and laughes at me.
So ever loose, so ever happy be.
But where so loose or happy that thou art,
Know, Marinell, that all this is for thee.'
With that she wept and wail'd, as if her hart
Would quite have burst through great abundance of her smart.

XII
All which complaint when Marinell had heard,
And understood the cause of all her care
To come of him, for using her so hard,
His stubborne heart, that never felt misfare,
Was toucht with soft remorse and pitty rare;
That even for griefe of minde he oft did grone,
And inly wish that in his powre it weare

Her to redresse: but since he meanes found none,
He could no more but her great misery bemone.

XIII
Thus whilst his stony heart with tender ruth
Was toucht, and mighty courage mollifide,
Dame Venus sonne, that tameth stubborne youth
With iron bit, and maketh him abide,
Till like a victor on his backe he ride,
Into his mouth his maystring bridle threw,
That made him stoupe, till he did him bestride:
Then gan he make him tread his steps anew,
And learne to love, by learning lovers paines to rew.

XIV
Now gan he in his grieved minde devise,
How from that dungeon he might her enlarge:
Some while he thought, by faire and humble wise
To Proteus selfe to sue for her discharge;
But then he fear'd his mothers former charge
Gainst womens love, long given him in vaine:
Then gan he thinke, perforce with sword and targe
Her forth to fetch, and Proteus to constraine;
But soone he gan such folly to forthinke againe.

XV
Then did he cast to steale her thence away,
And with him beare, where none of her might know.
But all in vaine: forwhy he found no way
To enter in, or issue forth below:
For all about that rocke the sea did flow.
And though unto his will she given were,
Yet without ship or bote her thence to row,
He wist not how her thence away to bere;
And daunger well he wist long to continue there.

XVI
At last when as no meanes he could invent,
Backe to him selfe he gan returne the blame,
That was the author of her punishment;
And with vile curses and reprochfull shame
To damne him selfe by every evill name;
And deeme unworthy or of love or life,
That had despisde so chast and faire a dame,
Which him had sought through trouble and long strife,
Yet had refusde a god that her had sought to wife.

XVII
In this sad plight he walked here and there,
And romed round about the rocke in vaine,
As he had lost him selfe, he wist not where;

Oft listening if he mote her heare againe,
And still bemoning her unworthy paine:
Like as an hynde whose calfe is falne unwares
Into some pit, where she him heares complaine,
An hundred times about the pit side fares,
Right sorrowfully mourning her bereaved cares.

XVIII
And now by this the feast was throughly ended,
And every one gan homeward to resort.
Which seeing, Marinell was sore offended,
That his departure thence should be so short,
And leave his love in that sea-walled fort.
Yet durst he not his mother disobay;
But her attending in full seemly sort,
Did march amongst the many all the way:
And all the way did inly mourne, like one astray.

XIX
Being returned to his mothers bowre,
In solitary silence far from wight,
He gan record the lamentable stowre
In which his wretched love lay day and night,
For his deare sake, that ill deserv'd that plight:
The thought whereof empierst his hart so deepe,
That of no worldly thing he tooke delight;
Ne dayly food did take, ne nightly sleepe,
But pyn'd, and mourn'd, and languisht, and alone did weepe;

XX
That in short space his wonted chearefull hew
Gan fade, and lively spirits deaded quight:
His cheeke bones raw, and eie-pits hollow grew,
And brawney armes had lost their knowen might,
That nothing like himselfe he seem'd in sight.
Ere long so weake of limbe, and sicke of love
He woxe, that lenger he note stand upright,
But to his bed was brought, and layd above,
Like ruefull ghost, unable once to stirre or move.

XXI
Which when his mother saw, she in her mind
Was troubled sore, ne wist well what to weene,
Ne could by search nor any meanes out find
The secret cause and nature of his teene,
Whereby she might apply some medicine;
But weeping day and night, did him attend,
And mourn'd to see her losse before her eyne,
Which griev'd her more that she it could not mend:
To see an helpelesse evill double griefe doth lend.

XXII
Nought could she read the roote of his disease,
Ne weene what mister maladie it is,
Whereby to seeke some meanes it to appease.
Most did she thinke, but most she thought amis,
That that same former fatall wound of his
Whyleare by Tryphon was not throughly healed,
But closely rankled under th' orifis:
Least did she thinke, that which he most concealed,
That love it was, which in his hart lay unrevealed.

XXIII
Therefore to Tryphon she againe doth hast,
And him doth chyde as false and fraudulent,
That fayld the trust which she in him bad plast,
To cure her sonne, as he his faith had lent:
Who now was falne into new languishment
Of his old hurt, which was not throughly cured.
So backe he came unto her patient:
Where searching every part, her well assured,
That it was no old sore which his new paine procured;

XXIV
But that it was some other maladie,
Or griefe unknowne, which he could not discerne:
So left he her withouten remedie.
Then gan her heart to faint, and quake, and earne,
And inly troubled was, the truth to learne.
Unto himselfe she came, and him besought,
Now with faire speches, now with threatnings sterne,
If ought lay hidden in his grieved thought,
It to reveale: who still her answered, there was nought.

XXV
Nathlesse she rested not so satisfide,
But leaving watry gods, as booting nought,
Unto the shinie heaven in haste she hide,
And thence Apollo, king of leaches, brought.
Apollo came; who, soone as he had sought
Through his disease, did by and by out find
That he did languish of some inward thought,
The which afflicted his engrieved mind;
Which love he red to be, that leads each living kind.

XXVI
Which when he had unto his mother told,
She gan thereat to fret and greatly grieve;
And comming to her sonne, gan first to scold
And chyde at him, that made her misbelieve:
But afterwards she gan him soft to shrieve,
And wooe with faire intreatie, to disclose

Which of the nymphes his heart so sore did mieve;
For sure she weend it was some one of those
Which he had lately seene, that for his love he chose.

XXVII
Now lesse she feared that same fatall read,
That warned him of womens love beware:
Which being ment of mortall creatures sead,
For love of nymphes she thought she need not care,
But promist him, what ever wight she weare,
That she her love to him would shortly gaine:
So he her told: but soone as she did heare
That Florimell it was, which wrought his paine,
She gan a fresh to chafe, and grieve in every vaine.

XXVIII
Yet since she saw the streight extremitie,
In which his life unluckily was layd,
It was no time to scan the prophecie,
Whether old Proteus true or false had sayd,
That his decay should happen by a mayd:
It's late, in death, of daunger to advize,
Or love forbid him that is life denayd:
But rather gan in troubled mind devize
How she that ladies libertie might enterprize.

XXIX
To Proteus selfe to sew she thought it vaine,
Who was the root and worker of her woe,
Nor unto any meaner to complaine;
But unto great King Neptune selfe did goe,
And on her knee before him falling lowe,
Made humble suit unto his Majestie,
To graunt to her her sonnes life, which his foe,
A cruell tyrant, had presumpteouslie
By wicked doome condemn'd a wretched death to die.

XXX
To whom God Neptune, softly smyling, thus:
'Daughter, me seemes of double wrong ye plaine,
Gainst one that hath both wronged you and us:
For death t' adward I ween'd did appertaine
To none but to the seas sole soveraine.
Read therefore who it is, which this hath wrought,
And for what cause; the truth discover plaine.
For never wight so evill did or thought,
But would some rightfull cause pretend, though rightly nought.'

XXXI
To whom she answerd: 'Then it is by name
Proteus, that hath ordayn'd my sonne to die;

For that a waift, the which by fortune came
Upon your seas, he clayrn'd as propertie:
And yet nor his, nor his in equitie,
But yours the waift by high prerogative.
Therefore I humbly crave your Majestie,
It to replevie, and my sonne reprive:
So shall you by one gift save all us three alive.'

XXXII
He graunted it: and streight his warrant made,
Under the sea-gods seale autenticall,
Commaunding Proteus straight t' enlarge the mayd
Which, wandring on his seas imperiall,
He lately tooke, and sithence kept as thrall.
Which grieved receiving with meete thankefulnesse,
Departed straight to Proteus therewithall:
Who, reading it with inward loathfulnesse,
Was grieved to restore the pledge he did possesse.

XXXIII
Yet durst he not the warrant to withstand,
But unto her delivered Florimell.
Whom she receiving by the lilly hand,
Admyr'd her beautie much, as she mote well;
For she all living creatures did excell;
And was right joyous, that she gotten had
So faire a wife for her sonne Marinell.
So home with her she streight the virgin lad,
And shewed her to him, then being sore bestad.

XXXIV
Who soone as he beheld that angels face,
Adorn'd with all divine perfection,
His cheared heart eftsoones away gan chace
Sad death, revived with her sweet inspection,
And feeble spirit inly felt refection;
As withered weed through cruell winters tine,
That feeles the warmth of sunny beames reflection,
Liftes up his head, that did before decline,
And gins to spread his leafe before the faire sunshine.

XXXV
Right so himselfe did Marinell upreare,
When he in place his dearest love did spy;
And though his limbs could not his bodie beare,
Ne former strength returne so suddenly,
Yet chearefull signes he shewed outwardly.
Ne lesse was she in secret hart affected,
But that she masked it with modestie,
For feare she should of lightnesse be detected:
Which to another place I leave to be perfected.

Edmund Spenser – A Short Biography

One of the greatest of English poets, Edmund Spenser was born in East Smithfield, London, in 1552, though an exact date is not recorded.

As a boy, he was educated in London at the Merchant Taylors' School and later at Pembroke College, Cambridge.

As a young man, in 1578, the young Edmund was, for a short time, secretary to John Young, the Bishop of Rochester.

In 1579, he published The Shepheardes Calender, his first major work. The poem follows Colin Clout, a folk character originated by John Skelton, and depicts his life as a shepherd through the twelve months of the year.

It is also around this time that Edmund was married for the first time to Machabyas Childe. The union produced two children; Sylvanus and Katherine.

Edmund journeyed to Ireland in July 1580, in the service of the newly appointed Lord Deputy, Arthur Grey, 14th Baron Grey de Wilton. His time included the terrible massacre at the Siege of Smerwick, though this event seems to have settled his views somewhat on Ireland and the Irish. (The Siege of Smerwick took place at Ard na Caithne in 1580, during the Second Desmond Rebellion. A 400–500 strong force of Papal soldiers captured the town but were later forced to retreat to nearby Dún an Óir, where they were besieged by the English Army and eventually surrendered. On the orders of the English Commander most were then massacred).

When Lord Grey was recalled to England, Edmund stayed, having being appointed to several other official posts and lands in the Munster Plantation. Between 1587 and 1589, Spenser acquired his main estate at Kilcolman, near Doneraile in North Cork.

He later bought a second holding to the south, at Rennie, on a rock overlooking the river Blackwater but still in North Cork. Its ruins are still visible today. A short distance away grew a tree, locally known as "Spenser's Oak". Local legend has it that he penned some of The Faerie Queene under this very tree.

This epic poem, The Faerie Queene, is acknowledged as Edmund's masterpiece. The first three books were published in 1590, and a second set of three books were published in 1596. The original idea was for the poem to consist of twelve books. So although the version we publish here is all that he actually wrote it is still one of the longest, and most magnificent, poems in English literature.

The Faerie Queene is a work on several levels of allegory, including as praise of Queen Elizabeth I. The poem follows several knights in an examination of several virtues. In Spenser's "A Letter of the Authors," he states that the entire epic poem is "cloudily enwrapped in allegorical devises," and that the aim behind The Faerie Queene was to "fashion a gentleman or noble person in virtuous and gentle discipline."

On its publication Spenser travelled to London to publish and promote the work. In this endeavour he was successful enough to obtain a life pension of £50 a year from the Queen who did not give these out lightly.

Spenser used a verse form, now called the Spenserian stanza, in The Faerie Queene as well as several others poems. The stanza's main meter is iambic pentameter with a final line in iambic hexameter (having six stresses, known as an Alexandrine). He was also to use his own rhyme scheme for the sonnet. In a Spenserian sonnet, the last line of every stanza is linked with the first line of the next one.

Spenser was well read in classical literature and strove to emulate such Roman poets as Virgil and Ovid, whom he had studied during his schooling.

Indeed the reality is that Spenser, through his great talents, was able to move Poetry in a different direction. It led to him being called a Poet's Poet and brought rich admiration from Milton, Raleigh, Blake, Wordsworth, Keats, Byron, and Lord Tennyson, among others. John Milton in his Areopagitica called Spenser "our sage and serious poet . . . whom I dare be known to think a better teacher than Scotus or Aquinas".

He had hoped this praise and pension might lead to a position at Court but his next work antagonised the queen's principal secretary, Lord Burghley, through the inclusion of the satirical Mother Hubberd's Tale.

Spenser returned to Ireland and in 1591, Complaints, a collection of poems that voices complaints in mournful or mocking tones was published.

By 1594, Spenser's first wife, Machabyas, had died. Very soon he married Elizabeth Boyle, and to which he dedicated the sonnet sequence Amoretti. The marriage itself was celebrated in Epithalamion and the fruit of this relationship was a son, Peregrine.

In 1595, Spenser now published Amoretti and Epithalamion. The volume contains eighty-nine sonnets.

In the following year Spenser released Prothalamion, a wedding song written for the daughters of a duke, allegedly in hopes to gain favour in the court. More importantly he also wrote a prose pamphlet titled A View of the Present State of Ireland (A Veue of the Present State of Irelande). It was circulated in manuscript form due to its highly inflammatory content. Its main argument was that Ireland would never be totally 'pacified' by the English until its indigenous language and customs had been destroyed, if necessary by violence.

Spenser was a strong proponent of, and wished devoutly, that the Irish language should be eradicated, writing that if children learn Irish before English, "Soe that the speach being Irish, the hart must needes be Irishe; for out of the aboundance of the hart, the tonge speaketh".

He further discussed in the pamphlet future draconian plans to subjugate Ireland, after the most recent rising, led by Hugh O'Neill, having again shown the failure of previous efforts. The work is also a partial defence of Lord Arthur Grey de Wilton, with whom Spenser previously served and who deeply influenced Spenser's views on Ireland.

The goal of this piece was to show that Ireland was in great need of reform. Spenser believed that "Ireland is a diseased portion of the State, it must first be cured and reformed, before it could be in a position to appreciate the good sound laws and blessings of the nation". Spenser categorises the "evils" of the Irish people into three distinct categories: laws, customs, and religion. These three elements work together in creating the disruptive and degraded people. One example given in the work is the native law system called "Brehon Law" which trumps the established law given by the English monarchy. This system has its own court and way of dealing with troubles. It has been passed down through the generations and Spenser views this system as a native and backward custom which must be destroyed. (As an example the Brehon Law methods of dealing with murder by imposing an éraic, or fine, on the murderer's whole family particularly horrified the English, in whose Protestant view a murderer should die for his act.)

He pressed for a scorched earth policy in Ireland, noting that the destruction of crops and animals had been successful in crushing the Second Desmond Rebellion of which he was a part.

However in 1598, during the Nine Years War, Spenser was, ironically, driven from his home by the native Irish forces of Aodh Ó Néill. His castle at Kilcolman was burned.

In 1599, Spenser travelled to London, where he died on January 13th at the age of forty-six. According to Ben Jonson, in another and tragic irony it was "for want of bread".

Edmund Spenser's coffin was carried to his grave in Westminster Abbey by other poets, who threw many pens and pieces of poetry into his grave followed with many tears.

His second wife, Elizabeth, survived him and went on to remarry twice.

Spenser was called a Poets' Poet and was admired by John Milton, William Blake, William Wordsworth, John Keats, Lord Byron, and Alfred Lord Tennyson, among others. Walter Raleigh wrote a dedicatory poem to The Faerie Queene in 1590, in which he claims to admire and value Spenser's work more so than any other in the English language. John Milton in his Areopagitica called Spenser "our sage and serious poet . . . whom I dare be known to think a better teacher than Scotus or Aquinas".

It is praise indeed and clearly shows why Edmund Spenser is indeed part of the Pantheon of our greatest Poets.

Edmund Spenser – A Concise Bibliography

1569 - Jan van der Noodt's A theatre for Worldlings, including poems translated into English by Spenser from French sources.

1579 - The Shepheardes Calender, published under the pseudonym "Immerito".

1580 - Three proper, and wittie, familar letters

1590 - The Faerie Queene, Books I–III

1591 - Complaints, Containing sundrie small Poemes of the Worlds Vanitie

1592 - Axiochus, a translation of a pseudo-Platonic dialogue from the original Ancient Greek; attributed to "Edw: Spenser" but the attribution is uncertain

1592 - Daphnaïda. An Elegy upon the death of the noble and vertuous Douglas Howard, Daughter and heire of Henry Lord Howard, Viscount Byndon, and wife of Arthure Gorges Esquier

1595 - Amoretti and Epithalamion

1595 - Astrophel. A Pastorall Elegie vpon the death of the most Noble and valorous Knight, Sir Philip Sidney.

1595 - Colin Clouts Come home againe

1596 - Four Hymns (poem)|Fowre Hymnes dedicated from the court at Greenwich.

1596 - Prothalamion

1596 - The Faerie Queene, Books IV-VI

1598 - A Veue of the Present State of Irelande (Manuscript)

1599 - Babel, Empress of the East – a dedicatory poem prefaced to Lewes Lewkenor's The Commonwealth of Venice.

1609 - Two Cantos of Mutabilitie published together with a reprint of The Fairie Queene.

1611 - First folio edition of Spenser's collected works

1633 - A Veue of the Present State of Irelande, a prose treatise on the reformation of Ireland.

www.ingramcontent.com/pod-product-compliance
Lightning Source LLC
Chambersburg PA
CBHW061443040426
42450CB00007B/1189